THE PIANOFORTE SONATA

THE PIANOFORTE SONATA

ITS ORIGIN AND DEVELOPMENT

BY

J. S. SHEDLOCK

With a Foreword to the Da Capo Edition by

WILLIAM S. NEWMAN

Alumni Distinguished Professor of Music
The University of North Carolina

Da Capo Press
NEW YORK
1964

A Da Capo Reprint Edition

Library of Congress Catalog Card Number: 64-18993

Printed in the United States of America

Foreword
to the
Da Capo Edition

At first thought it has always seemed surprising that among the many thousands upon thousands of books on music that have appeared over nearly five centuries of printing, such an infinitesimally few have made primary, frontal attacks on music's most basic elements, processes, and forms. Aside from essentially pedagogic publications, you can still count on the fingers of one hand the number of comprehensive treatises on rhythmic organization, or phrase syntax, or textural variety, or style differentiation, or almost any of the main form types through the ages. Of course, on second thought the reason is not hard to guess. The most basic, over-all problems are also the most elusive ones. The broad answers to them can come only after the details first have been gathered along the way, then digested, reconciled, and assimilated.

As a form type that has yielded some of the grandest architectures in absolute music, the sonata is a case in point. Until recently no comprehensive survey of its history, from its sixteenth-century origins to the present day, had been undertaken. Indeed, in my own publications leading to a "History of the Sonata Idea" I have claimed as their first justification the simple fact of that conspicuous gap in music literature. At the same time, I hope I have pointed with sufficient emphasis to *The Pianoforte Sonata* by John South Shedlock (1843-1919), written some seventy years ago, as "the single best start toward a general view of the sonata" since the first historical article on the subject appeared about 125 years ago.

Shedlock's book was originally published by Methuen & Co. of London in 1895. Before it, C. F. Becker had published an article (1837) on Kuhnau as the "first" composer of keyboard sonatas, Imanuel Faisst had done a doctoral dissertation (1845) on the keyboard sonata up to Emanuel Bach, C. H. H. Parry had written the thirty-page article on the "Sonata" for the first edition (1878-89) of *Grove's Dictionary* that still appears with but few changes and additions in the recent fifth edition (1954), and a few less consequential publications had appeared. It is noteworthy that within two years after its original publication, Shedlock's book was translated and published in Germany, the land from which most of the general and special contributions on the sonata have come. Two years later (1899) Otto Klauwell published his little *Geschichte der Sonate,* which leans heavily on Shedlock and certain German studies of more restricted scope. A few other books and articles of a general nature appeared on the sonata after Klauwell's book, but none at the level of distinction of Shedlock's book.

Shedlock's book deserves this reprinting in spite of the shortcomings and errors to be expected in a pioneer survey. After all, it preceded nearly all the important monographs or other specialized publications that have dealt with the sonata, and there have been many of these since the turn of the century. Perhaps it would be well to dispose of the shortcomings and errors first. Shedlock's errors of fact are neither many nor careless. They are largely the sort that have been corrected since his day by the discovery of new or better information. For instance, many sources still repeat the old error of 1683 for the date of the first edition of Corelli's Opus 1 (as on p. 12), instead of the 1681 that is printed clearly enough on the score. The concept of Scarlatti's sonatas as being primarily in one movement (p. 15) still persists in spite of their grouping in two or more movements in the earliest extant copies, as first noted by Gerstenberg in 1933. Sandoni's sonatas were published in London not in 1721 (p. 23) but between 1726 and 1728. Haydn left not thirty-five known keyboard sonatas (p. 113) but at least forty-nine that can be confirmed.

The shortcomings in Shedlock's book result partly from the fact that it appeared before nearly all the dating and bibliographic aids and nearly all the special studies in depth had been made available to historians, and partly because the historical views themselves have changed so greatly today. The first shortcoming is also reflected in the limited range of sonatas examined by the author. Like Parry and like his German contemporaries he found his earlier keyboard examples primarily—though,

VIII   Foreword to the Da Capo Edition

be it said to his credit, not entirely—among the sonatas made available in the "Old Masters" anthologies that Louis Köhler and Ernst Pauer had first published. Subsequent favorites like the sonatas of Platti, Soler, or Hüllmandel pass without mention. And, of course, we must remember that Shedlock could hardly carry the sonata beyond the "moderns" of his own day. Liszt and Brahms are his most recent masters of the sonata, while Heller, Raff, Rubinstein, Bargiel, and Grieg are his still later composers of "still more modern works."

As for historical attitudes, above all Shedlock was representative of his day in being an "evolutionalist." Like Parry, Hadow, Klauwell, Bie, and many a writer since, he concerned himself primarily with the tracing of the "evolution" of "sonata form." In fact, it is not going too far to say that he chose or emphasized just those examples—meaning, usually, those first movements—that illustrated and fell in with a logical, preconceived development of "sonata form." The presence and distinctness of a "second theme," or a "development section," or a recapitulation become the main criteria for historical "progress," although these elements actually remained among the most flexible traits of "sonata form" throughout the Classic Era. The same historical views would help to explain why a composer as relatively unimportant to the history of the keyboard sonata as Kuhnau takes up nearly a seventh of the whole book!

Yet, with all these reservations Shedlock's book remains a worthwhile, highly readable account. One expects no less when the author is a man of such genuine cultural interests, refreshing musical enjoyments, and considerable research skill. The chapter on Kuhnau may be disproportionate and overly enthusiastic. But if anything it makes even more informative, entertaining reading on that account. Richly illustrated with music examples and translated inscriptons, it still provides, in fact, one of the most useful discussions of Kuhnau's contribution. The same may be said for the eleven pages on Bernardo Pasquini, which represents firsthand research by Shedlock in conjunction with his edition of an anthology of Pasquini keyboard pieces (Novello, *ca.* 1895). We also get the benefit and interest of firsthand contacts when Shedlock writes on Beethoven and incorporates his special studies of the composer's sketchbooks as well as his translator's close knowledge of the letters. And Shedlock's penultimate chapter on "The Sonata in England" naturally affords a close view not obtainable by writers who were not on the scene. Even when he was not doing original spadework, the author must be credited with going always to the best sources then available, such as Bitter on Bach's sons or Jahn on Mozart.

This little introduction might well end with at least seventy years' worth of answer to the question on which Shedlock ends the main body of his book (p. 220): "Is Liszt's sonata a Phoenix rising from its ashes? Shall we be able to say 'La sonate est morte! Vive la sonate!' Time will tell. Hitherto Liszt's work has not borne fruit."

From today's vantage point the answer must be that, whether the fruit derives from Liszt or not, the perdurable sonata is by no means dead yet. Claude Debussy, Maurice Ravel, Darius Milhaud, Béla Bartók, Arthur Shepherd, Ernest Bloch, Aaron Copland, Paul Hindemith, Sergey Prokofiev, Arnold Bax, Ralph Vaughan Williams, Charles Griffes, and Samuel Barber are but a few of those who have kept it alive and healthy, and there is no abatement of new young composers to continue its substantial nurture.

WILLIAM S. NEWMAN

THE UNIVERSITY OF NORTH CAROLINA

THE PIANOFORTE SONATA

MONUMENT OF BERNARDO PASQUINI

IN THE CHURCH OF SAN LORENZO IN LUCINA ROME

SKETCHED BY STRITCH HUTTON

THE

PIANOFORTE SONATA

ITS ORIGIN AND DEVELOPMENT

J. S. SHEDLOCK, B.A.

METHUEN & CO.

36 ESSEX STREET, W.C.

LONDON

1895

PREFACE

THIS little volume is entitled "The Pianoforte Sonata: its Origin and Development." Some of the early sonatas mentioned in it were, however, written for instruments of the jack or tangent kind. Even Beethoven's sonatas up to Op. 27, inclusive, were published for "Clavicembalo o Pianoforte." The Germans have the convenient generic term "Clavier," which includes the old and the new instruments with hammer action; hence, they speak of a *Clavier Sonate* written, say, by Kuhnau, in the seventeenth, or of one by Brahms in the nineteenth, century.

The term "Piano e Forte" is, however, to be found in letters of a musical instrument maker named Paliarino, written, as we learn from the valuable article "Pianoforte," contributed by Mr. Hipkins to Sir George Grove's *Dictionary of*

Music and Musicians, already in the year 1598, and addressed to Alfonso II., Duke of Modena. The earliest sonata for a keyed instrument mentioned in this volume was published in 1695; and to avoid what seems an unnecessary distinction, I have used the term " Pianoforte Sonata " for that sonata and for some other works which followed, and which are usually and properly termed " Harpsichord Sonatas."

I have to acknowledge kind assistance received from Mr. A. W. Hutton, Mr. F. G. Edwards, and Mr. E. Van der Straeten. And I also beg to thank Mr. W. Barclay Squire and Mr. A. Hughes-Hughes for courteous help at the British Museum; likewise Dr. Kopfermann, chief librarian of the musical section of the Berlin Royal Library.

J. S. SHEDLOCK.

LONDON, 1895.

CONTENTS

THE PIANOFORTE SONATA

—◆—

CHAPTER I

INTRODUCTORY

IN history we find certain names associated with great movements: Luther with the Reformation, or Garibaldi with the liberation of Italy. Luther certainly posted on the door of the church at Wittenberg his famous Theses, and burnt the Papal Bull at the gates of that city; yet before Luther there lived men, such as the scholar Erasmus, who have been appropriately named Reformers before the Reformation. So, too, Cavour's cautious policy paved the way for Garibaldi's brilliant victories. Once again, Leonardo da Vinci is named as the inventor of chiaroscuro, yet he was preceded by Fra Filippo Lippi. And in similar manner, in music, certain men are associated with certain forms. Haydn, for example, is called the father of the quartet; close investigation, however, would show that he was only a link, and certainly not the first one in a long evolution. So, too, with the sonata. The present volume is, however, specially concerned with the *clavier* or pianoforte sonata; and for that we have a convenient starting-point—the Sonata in B flat of Kuhnau, published in 1695. The date is easy to remember, for in that same year died England's greatest musician, Henry Purcell.

Before studying the history of the pianoforte sonata, even in outline, it is essential that something should be said about the early history of the *sonata*. That term appears first to have been used in contradistinction to *cantata*: the one was a piece *sounded* (*suonata*, from *sonando*) by instruments; the other, one *sung* by voices. The form of these early sonatas (as they appear in Giovanni Gabrieli's works towards the close of the sixteenth century) was vague; yet, in spite of light imitations, the basis was harmonic, rather than contrapuntal. They were among the first fruits of the Renaissance in Italy. But soon there came about a process of differentiation. Praetorius, in his *Syntagma musicum*, published at Wolfenbüttel in 1619, distinguishes between the *sonata* and the *canzona*. Speaking generally, from the one seems to have come the sonata proper; from the other, the suite. During the whole of the eighteenth century there was a continual intercrossing of these two species; it is no easy matter, therefore, to trace the early stages of development of each separately.

Marpurg, in his description of various kinds of pieces in his *Clavierstücke*, published at Berlin in

1762, says: "Sonatas are pieces in three or four movements, marked merely *Allegro, Adagio, Presto,* etc., although in character they may be really an *Allemande, Courante,* and *Gigue.*" Corelli, as will be mentioned later on, gave dance titles in addition to Allegro, Adagio, etc. Marpurg also states that "when the middle movement is in slow time it is not always in the key of the first and last movements." This, again, shows intercrossing. The genuine suite consisted of several dance movements (Allemande, Courante, Sarabande, Gigue) all in the same key. But we find occasionally in suites, a Fugue or Fuguetta, or even an Aria or Adagio; and in name, at any rate, one dance movement has formed part of the sonata since the time of Emanuel Bach.

In 1611, Banchieri, an Olivetan monk, published at Venice his *L'Organo suonarino,* a work "useful and necessary to organists,"—thus runs the title-page. At the end of the volume there are some pieces, vocal and instrumental (a Concerto for soprano or tenor, with organ, a Fantasia, Ricercata, etc.), among which are to be found two *sonatas,* the one entitled, " Prima Sonata, doppio soggietto," the other "Seconda Sonata, soggietto triplicato." They are written out in open score of four staves, with mezzo-soprano, alto, tenor, and bass clefs. To show how the sonatas of those days differed both in form and contents from the sonata of our century, the first of the above-mentioned is given in short score. It will, probably, remind readers of "the first (*i.e.* sonatas) that my (*i.e.* Dr. Burney) musical inquiries have discovered, viz., some sonatas by Francesco Turini, which consisted of only a single movement, in fugue and imitation throughout."

Turini was organist of Brescia Cathedral, and in 1624 published *Madrigali a una, due, tre voci, con alcune Sonate e a tre, Ven. 1624.* Between

Turini, also Carlo Farina, who published violin sonatas at Dresden in 1628, and Corelli (*b.* 1653), who brought out his first work in 1683, one name of great importance is Giovanni Legrenzi.

In the eighth volume of Dr. Burney's musical extracts there are two sonatas, *a tre, a due violini e violone,* by Legrenzi (opera ottava, 1677). The first is in B flat. It commences with a movement in common time entitled *La Benivoglia.*

An Adagio in G minor (only six bars) is followed by an Allegro in D minor, six-eight time, closing on a major chord; then eight bars common time in B flat (no heading); and, finally, a Presto (three-four) commencing in G minor and closing in B flat. None of the movements is in binary form.

The 2nd Sonata, in D, has five short movements. No. 1 has an opening of thirty-seven bars in common time, fugato. There is a modulation in the ninth bar to the dominant, and, later on, a return to the opening theme and key; in the intervening space, however, in spite of modulation, the principal key is not altogether avoided.

Sonatas of various kinds by Legrenzi appeared between 1655 and 1677. Then there were the "Varii Fiori del Giardino Musicale ouero Sonate da Camera, etc.," of Gio. Maria Bononcini, father of Battista Bononcini, the famous rival of Handel, published at Bologna in 1669, and the sonatas of

Gio. Battista Vitali (Bologna, 1677). Giambatista Bassani of Bologna, although his junior by birth, was the violin master of the great Corelli. His sonatas only appeared after those of his illustrious pupil, yet may have been composed before. Of the twelve in Op. 5, most have many short movements; some, indeed, are so short as to be scarcely deserving of the name.

By the time of Arcangelo Corelli, who, as mentioned, published his first work (Op. 1, twelve sonatas for two violins and a bass) in 1683, sonatas answered to the definition given by Mattheson in his *Das neu eröffnete Orchester* (1713), in which they are said to consist of alternate Adagio and Allegro. J. G. Walther, again, in his dictionary of music,[1] which appeared at Leipzig in 1732, describes a sonata as a " grave artistic composition for instruments, especially violins." The idea of grouping movements was already in vogue in the sixteenth century. Morley in his *Plain and Easy Introduction to Practical Music*, printed in 1597, speaks of the desirableness of *alternating* Pavans and Galliards, the one being " a kind of staid musick ordained for grave dancing," and the other " a lighter and more stirring kind of dancing." Contrast was obtained, too, not only by difference in the character, but also, in the measure of the music; the former was in common, the latter in triple time.

With regard to the grouping of movements, Corelli's sonatas show several varieties. The usual

[1] *Musikalisches Lexicon oder musikalische Bibliothek.*

number, however, was four, and the order generally—
slow, fast, slow, fast. Among the forty-eight (Op.
1, 2, 3, and 4, published 1685, 1690, 1694, and 1700
respectively) we find the majority in four movements,
in the order given above[1]; of the twelve in Op. 3,
no less than eleven have four movements, but—

No. 1 (in F) has	Grave, Allegro, Vivace, Allegro.
No. 6 (in G),	Vivace, Grave, Allegro, Allegro.
No. 10 (in A minor),	Vivace, Allegro, Adagio, Allegro.

There are, however, eight sonatas consisting of
three movements; and as this, a century later, became the normal number, we will give the list :—

Op. 1, No. 7 (in C)	Allegro, Grave, Allegro.
	(Middle movement begins in A minor, but ends in C.)
Op. 2, No. 2 (in D minor)	Allemanda (Adagio)
	Corrente (Allegro), Giga (Allegro).
Op. 2, No. 6 (in G minor)	Allemanda (Largo), Corrente, Giga.
Op. 2, No. 9 (F sharp minor)	Allemanda (Largo).
	Tempo di Sarabanda (Largo).
	Giga (Allegro).
Op. 4, No. 8 (D minor)	Preludio (Grave).
	Allemanda (Allegro).
	Sarabanda (Allegro).
Op. 4, No. 10 (G)	Preludio[2] (Adagio) and Allegro.
	Adagio and Grave (E minor).
	Tempo di Gavotta (Allegro).

---

[1] Among the four-movement sonatas of Op. 1, No. 6 (in B minor)
has the peculiar order : Grave, Largo, Adagio, Allegro.

[2] The Preludio Adagio only consists of four chords, or two bars ;
the Adagio, again, only consists of four bars. The sonata,
therefore, may be considered as of three movements.

Op. 4, No. 11 (C minor)	Preludio (Largo).
	Corrente (Allegro).
	Allemanda (Allegro).
Op. 4, No. 12 (B minor)	Preludio (Largo).
	Allemanda (Presto).
	Giga (Allegro).

It is interesting to note that each of the two sonatas (Op. 1, No. 7, and Op. 4, No. 10), most in keeping with its title of sonata, has the middle movement in a relative key. Op. 1, No. 7, begins with an Allegro in common time; and the short Grave is followed by a light Allegro in six-eight time. The first movement, with its marked return to the principal key, is very interesting in the matter of form. The other sonatas with suite titles have all their movements in the same key. Locatelli in his *XII Sonate* for flute, published early in the eighteenth century, has in the first: Andante, Adagio, Presto; also Nos. 3, 5, etc. So, too, in Tartini's Sonatas (Op. 1) there are also some in three (No. 3, etc.). But Emanuel Bach commenced with that number, to which, with few and unimportant exceptions, he remained faithful; likewise to the slow movement dividing the two quick ones. The three-movement form used by J. S. Bach for his concertos and sonatas no doubt considerably influenced his son. But already, in 1668, Diderich Becker, in his *Musikalische Frülings-Früchte*, wrote sonatas for violins, etc. and *continuo*, in three movements. (No. 10, Allegro, Adagio, Allegro. Again, Sonata No. 19 opens with a

movement in common time, most probably an
Allegro; then comes an Adagio, and, lastly, a
movement in six-four, most probably quick *tempo*.)
These sonatas of Becker *a 3, 4* or *5*, with *basso
continuo*, are unfortunately only printed in parts.
As a connecting link between the Gabrielis and
Corelli, and more particularly as a forerunner
of Kuhnau, Becker is of immense importance.
We are concerned with the clavier sonata,
otherwise we should certainly devote more space
to this composer. We have been able to trace
back sonatas by German composers to Becker
(1668), and by Italian composers to Legrenzi
(1655); those of Gabrieli and Banchieri, as
short pieces, not a group of movements, are not
taken into account. Now, of earlier history, we do
know that Hans Leo. von Hasler, said to have
been born at Nuremberg in 1564, studied first with
his father, but afterwards at Venice, and for a whole
year under A. Gabrieli. Italian and German art
are thus intimately connected; but what each gave
to, or received from, the other with regard to
the sonata seems impossible to determine. The
Becker sonatas appeared at Hamburg, and surely
E. Bach must have been acquainted with them.
Becker in his preface mentions another Hamburg
musician—a certain Johann Schop—who did much
for the cause of instrumental music. Schop, it
appears, published concertos for various instruments already in the year 1644. And there was
still another work of importance published at

INTRODUCTION

Amsterdam, very early in the eighteenth century, by the famous violinist and composer G. Torelli, which must have been known to E. Bach. It is entitled "Six Sonates ou Concerts à 4, 5, e 6 Parties," and of these, five have three movements (Allegro, Adagio, and Allegro).

Corelli was the founder of a school of violin composers, of which Geminiani,[1] Locatelli,[2] Veracini,[3] and Tartini[4] were the most distinguished representatives; the first two were actually pupils of the master. In the sonatas of these men there is an advance in two directions: sonata-form[5] is in process of evolution from binary form, *i.e.* the second half of the first section is filled with subject-matter of more definite character; the bars of modulation and development are growing in number and importance; and the principal theme appears as the commencement of a recapitulation. We should like to say that *binary* is changing into

---

[1] 1680-1762.   [2] 1693-1764.

[3] 1685-1750 (Veracini is regarded as of the Corelli school, yet it should not be forgotten that his uncle, Antonio Veracini, is said to have published "Sonate a tre, due violini e violone, o arciliuto col basso continuo per l'organo" at Florence, already in 1662).

[4] 1692-1770

[5] It is important to distinguish between *sonata* and *sonata-form*. The first movement of a modern sonata is usually in sonata-form; but there are sonatas (Beethoven, Op. 26, etc.) which contain no such movement. Sonata-form, as will be shown later on, has been evolved from old binary form. By *sonata* is understood merely a group of movements; hence objection may certainly be taken to the term as applied to the one-movement pieces of Dom. Scarlatti, which are not even in sonata-form.

ternary form; unfortunately, however, the latter
term is used for a different kind of movement.
To speak of a movement in sonata-form, containing three sections (exposition, development, and
recapitulation) as in binary form, seems a decided
misnomer.

The violinists just mentioned were the last
great writers of sonatas in Italy. Emanuel Bach
arose during the first half of the eighteenth century,
and, henceforth, Germany took the lead; Bach was
followed by Haydn, Mozart, and Beethoven.
The influence of the Corelli[1] school was felt in
Germany and also in England. Sonatas were
published by Veracini at Dresden in 1721, and by
Tartini and Locatelli at Amsterdam before 1740.
Again Veracini was for a time solo violinist to the
Elector of Dresden (1720–23); Tartini lived for
three years at Prague (1723–26), while Locatelli,
during the first half of the eighteenth century, made
frequent journeys throughout Germany. Emanuel
Bach, the real founder of the modern pianoforte
sonata, must have been influenced by their works.

In a history of the development of the sonata
generally, those of Corelli would occupy an
important place, for in them we find not only
fugal and dance forms, but also hints of sonata-
form.

Dr. Parry, in his article on " Sonata " in Sir G.

---

[1] It must be remembered that Corelli spent some time in Germany
between 1680 and 1683, the latter being the year of publication of
his first sonatas at Rome.

Grove's *Dictionary of Music and Musicians,* has named the Corrente of Corelli's 5th Sonata in Op. 4 as offering "nearly a miniature of modern binary form." The well-known Giga Allegro of the 9th Sonata (Op. 5), and the Allemanda Allegro of the 10th Concerto in C, also present remarkable foreshadowings.

Handel, however, furnishes a very striking illustration—

In the six "Sonatas or Trios for two Hoboys with a thorough bass for the harpischord," said to have been composed already in 1696, we find quick movements in binary form. In some, the first section offers both a first and a second subject, while in the second section, after modulation, there is a return to the opening theme, though quite at the close of that section. A brief description of one will make the form clearer. The second Allegro of No. 4 (in F) has two sections. The first, which ends in the dominant key (C), contains forty-six bars. The opening theme begins thus :—

At the twenty-ninth bar, a passage leads to the second theme—

This second theme is, in a measure, evolved from the first. In any case, it is of subordinate character ; and it differs slightly as given by first or second oboe, whereas the principal theme appears in exactly the same manner for both instruments.

The second section opens with developments of *b*, and modulation from C major to D minor; *a* also is developed, the music passing from the last-named key back to the opening one. There is a full close in that key, and then modulation to F. The remaining twenty-two bars give the first section in condensed form: first and second subjects and coda.[1]

It would be interesting to trace the influences acting on the youth Handel at the time when he wrote these sonatas. Most probably they were Johann Philipp Krieger's[2] sonatas for violins and bass; N. A. Strungk's sonatas published at Dresden in 1691; and more especially Agostino Steffani's "Sonate da Camera" for two violins, alto, and bass, published in 1683. An opera by the last-named, which appeared at Hanover in 1699, has an "Air de Ballet," which contains the first notes of "Let the bright Seraphim"; besides, it is known that Handel culled ideas and "conveyed" notes from works of other composers; also, that he turned them to the best account.

[1] In J. S. Bach's 2nd Sonata for Flauto traverso and Cembalo (third movement) there is a return to the opening theme in the second section; also in the Presto of the sonata for two violins and figured bass we have an example very similar to the "Hoboy" sonata of Handel.

[2] Krieger, by the way, studied under Bernardo Pasquini at Rome.

In the same year in which Corelli published his
Op. 1 (1683), Domenico Scarlatti, the famous
harpsichord player, was probably born; in the
history of development his name is the principal one
of importance between Corelli and Emanuel Bach.
In the matter of technique he rendered signal
service, but, for the moment, we are concerned with
his contribution towards development. Scarlatti
does not seem to have ever considered the sonata
in the sense of a work consisting of several con-
trasting movements; all of his are of only one
movement. The title " sonata " as applied to his
pieces is, therefore, misleading. Whether the
term was actually used by the composer himself
seems doubtful. The first thirty of the sixty
Scarlatti sonatas published by Breitkopf & Härtel
appeared during the lifetime of the composer at
Madrid. They are dedicated to John the Just,
King of Portugal, and are merely entitled

Essercizi per Gravicembalo.

In editions of the eighteenth century the
composer's pieces are styled Lessons or Suites.
However, twelve published by J. Johnson, London, are described on the title-page as *Sonatas
modernas*.

From the earliest days of instrumental music
dance tunes were divided into two sections. The
process of evolution is interesting. In the earliest
specimens, such as the *Branle* given in the Orché-

sographie of Thoinot Arbeau, we find both sections in the same key, and there is only one
theme. The movement towards the dominant
note in this *Branle* may be regarded as a latent
modulation. In time the first section was developed, and the latent modulation became real; then,
after certain intermediate stages, the custom was
established of passing from the principal to the
dominant key (or, in a minor piece, to the relative
major or dominant minor), in which the first section closed. But in Corelli,[1] and even in Scarlatti,[2]
we find, occasionally, a return to an earlier stage
(*i.e.* a first section ending in the same key in
which it commenced). In most of his pieces
Scarlatti modulates to the dominant; in minor,
to the relative major. Some exceptions deserve
mention. In the Breitkopf & Härtel collection,
No. 26, in A major, passes to the minor key of
the dominant; and No. 11, in C minor, modulates
to the minor key of the dominant, but the section
closes in the major key of the dominant.

Scarlatti's sonatas consist, then, of one movement in binary form of the early type. Only in
a few of these pieces is there a definite second
subject; in none, a return to the
opening theme. In No. 26 there
is just a return to the first bar

Presto.   *tr*

[1] Cf. Corelli : Corrente in 10th Sonata of Op. 2 ; also Allemande
and Giga of the next sonata.

[2] Cf. Scarlatti : No. 10 of the sixty sonatas published by Breitkopf
& Härtel.

(see second section, bar 11), but the previous ten bars show no modulation, and one can scarcely speak of thematic development. After the few bars of development and modulation, in some cases, the second section is found to consist merely of a repetition of some part of the first section, the key being tonic instead of dominant. This is, practically, embryonic sonata-form. The tonic and dominant portions of the first section are becoming differentiated; but the landmark, *i.e.* the return to the opening theme in the second section which divides binary from sonata form, is, in Scarlatti, non-existent. His first sections often consist of a principal theme and passages, also phrases indirectly connected with the opening one; sometimes of a chain of short phrases more or less evolved from the opening thought (see Nos. 1, 21, 29). (These and the numbers which follow refer to the Breitkopf & Härtel edition of sixty Scarlatti sonatas.) The composer often passes through the minor key of the dominant (in the first section) before arriving at the major; sometimes the major is introduced only late in the section (Nos. 7, 17, etc.), or minor remains (No. 26). We meet with a similar proceeding in Beethoven. Minor pieces often pass to the dominant minor, but end in major (*i.e.*, first section). In Scarlatti there is, for the most part, no second subject, but frequently (Nos. 5, 7, 9, etc.) a concluding phrase which can, at times, be traced to the opening theme. Sonata 6, in F, shows a second subject

of a certain independence. The best examples
are to be found in Nos. 24 and 29 (in A and E);
in these the character of the second subject differs
from that of the first, and it is also in a minor key,
which offers still another contrast.

And now a word or two respecting Scarlatti's
method of development. He alters figures (Nos.
12 and 54), extends them (Nos. 9 and 54), but
often merely repeats passages on the same degrees
as those of the first section, or on different ones.
He makes use of imitation (Nos. 7 and 36). Sometimes he evolves a phrase from a motive (No. 11).
In No. 19 the development assumes a certain importance. It commences, not, as in most cases, with
the opening theme or figure of the first section, but
with a group of semiquaver notes which appears later
in that section. In No. 20 Scarlatti preserves the
rhythm, but with total change of notes (No. 20)—

The same number gives another interesting specimen of change of rhythm. In No. 48 he picks
out an unimportant group of notes, and works it
by imitation and sequence. There are some interesting specimens of development in the thirty
sonatas printed from manuscripts in the possession
of Lord Viscount Fitzwilliam by Robert Birchall.
Scarlatti's development bars are seldom many in
number.

After modulation and development, the music slides, as it were, into some phrase from the first section,[1] and allowance being made on account of difference of key (there the music was passing, or had passed from tonic ; here it is returning to that key), the rest is more or less a repetition of the first section. *More or less*: sometimes the repetition is literal ; at other times there is considerable deviation ; and shortenings are frequent. With regard to style of writing for the clavier—a few canonic imitations excepted—there is no real polyphony. Most of the sonatas are in only two parts. The composer revels in rapid passages (runs, broken chords, simple and compound), wide leaps, difficult octaves, crossing of hands, and, of course, short shakes innumerable. Domenico Scarlatti was indeed one of the most renowned *virtuosi* on the clavier. Handel met him at Rome in 1708, and Cardinal Ottoboni persuaded them to compete with each other. We are told that upon the harpsichord the victory was doubtful, but upon the organ, Scarlatti himself confessed the superiority of his rival.[2]

Johann Kuhnau published a sonata for clavier in 1695, and this was followed up by a set of seven sonatas (" Frische Früchte") in 1696, and a few years later (1700) by the seven " Bible " Sonatas. That he was the first composer who

---

[1] When there is clearly a second subject, that of course offers the point of return. (See Nos. 24 and 29.)

[2] See V. Schœlcher's *Life of Handel*, p. 23.

wrote a sonata for the clavier is a point which
cannot be overlooked, and in the evolution of the
sonata he occupies an interesting position.   In the
"Frische Früchte" there is, as Dr. C. H. Parry truly
remarks in his excellent article " Sonata " in Sir
G. Grove's *Dictionary of Music and Musicians*, an
awakening sense of the relation and balance of
keys ; but in the " Bible " Sonatas the form and
order of the movements is entirely determined by
the Bible stories.   As specimens of programme-
music they are altogether remarkable, and will,
later on, be described in detail ; they do not,
however, come within the regular line of development.   It was, of course, natural that such a new
departure should attract the notice of John Sebastian Bach, who was Kuhnau's immediate successor
as cantor of St. Thomas' School, Leipzig, and
Spitta, in his life of Bach, refers to that composer's
*Capriccio sopra la lontananza del suo fratello dilet-
tissimo*, and reminds us that " Kuhnau as well as
so many others had some influence on Bach."   Of
course, among the " so many others," Froberger's
name—as we shall see later on from Kuhnau's
preface—deserves a prominent place.   In addition
to what Kuhnau says, Mattheson has recorded that
" Froberger could depict whole histories on the
clavier, giving a representation of the persons
present and taking part in them, with all their
natural characters."   When writing the Capriccio
above named, Spitta believes that Bach was specially
influenced by the last of the " Bible " Sonatas (we

may perhaps add that Spitta tells us that Bach was intimately acquainted with Kuhnau). He indeed says : " We might doubt the early origin of the Capriccio if its evident ' dependence ' on Kuhnau did not solve the mystery." Then, again, in a Sonata in D by Bach, published in the Bach Gesellschaft edition, Spitta calls attention to the opening subject in D, and does not hesitate to declare that " it is constructed on the pattern of a particular part of the story of Jacob's marriage (the 3rd of the "Bible" Sonatas). His description of the Bach sonata would, doubtless, have attracted more notice but for the fact that copies of the Kuhnau sonatas were extremely rare ; they were, we believe, never reprinted since the commencement of the eighteenth century. The first two have now been published by Messrs Novello & Co. The Kuhnau influence on Bach seems, however, to have been of short duration ; for, after these juvenile attempts, as Spitta observes, " he never again returned to this branch of music in the whole course of a long artistic career extending over nearly fifty years." The fugue form absorbed nearly the whole attention of that master ; and the idea of programme-music remained in abeyance until Beethoven revived it a century later.[1] Emanuel Bach inherited some of his father's genius, and he may instinctively have felt the utter hopelessness of following directly in his footsteps. J. S. Bach had exhausted the possibilities of the fugue form.

[1] See, however, chapter on the predecessors of Beethoven.

It was perhaps fortunate for Emanuel Bach that, while still young, he left his father's house.   After residing for a few years at Frankfort-on-the-Oder, he entered the service of Frederick the Great ; and at the court of that monarch he came, at any rate, directly under Italian influence.

An interesting link between Kuhnau and E Bach is Mattheson, who published at Hamburg in 1713 a sonata dedicated to the one who can best play it (*derjenigen Persohn gewidmet, die sie am besten spielen wird*).   The work itself not being available, the following description of it by J. Faisst (*Caecilia*, vol. 25, p. 157) may prove interesting :—
" It (*i.e.* the sonata) consists of only one movement, which, considering its evidently intentional wealth of technique, might be named a Toccata.   But in form this one movement clearly belongs to the sonata order, and, in fact, holds a middle place between the tendencies towards sonata-form (the term taken in the narrower sense of form of one single move-ment) noticeable in Kuhnau, and the more developed shape which this form has assumed within recent times.   We have here three sections.   In the opening one, the theme, after its first exposition in the key of G, forms the basis of various passages, and then appears in the key of the dominant, followed again by passages of larger extent and richer contents ; finally, in abbreviated form, it reappears in the tonic.   The second section commences in the parallel key, E minor, with passages which recall those of the first section, and continues with the theme in

the same key ; afterwards theme and passages are
developed through the keys of A minor, C major, G
major, D major and B minor ; in the last, in which
the theme occurs, there is a full close. As third
section the first is taken *Da Capo*." It is evident
from a remark made by Mattheson in his *Der
volkommene Capellmeister*, which appeared at
Hamburg in 1739, that some of the sonatas written
during the transition period, between Corelli and
E. Bach, are lost, or, at any rate, have not been
discovered.[1] Mattheson says : " During the last
years successful attempts have been made to write
sonatas for the clavier (formerly they were for
violins or instruments of that kind) ; still, up to
now, they have not the right form, and are capable
of being touched (*i.e.* played) rather than of touching : they aim at the movement of fingers rather
than of hearts."[2]

A little later than Mattheson (*i.e.* in 1721), Pier
Giuseppo Sandoni, husband of the famous vocalist
Cuzzoni, published at London " Sonate per il
Cembalo," dedicated to the Duchess of Pembroke.
No. 1, in D minor, has three movements, an Alle-
mande, Largo, and Giga Presto ; they are all
short, and in two sections ; and, as a rule, the
writing is in two parts. No. 2, in F, opens with

[1] See ch. iii. on Pasquini.

[2] " Seit einigen Jahren hat man angefangen, Sonaten für's Clavier
(da sie sonst nur für Violinen u. dgl. gehören) mit gutem Beifall zu
setzen ; bisher haben sie noch die rechte Gestalt nicht, und wollen
mehr gerührt werden, als rühren, das ist, sie zielen mehr auf die
Bewegung der Finger als der Herzen."

an Allegro of peculiar form.   It has four sections,
each of which is repeated ; the first (seven bars)
modulates to the key of C, closing thus—

The second section (also consisting of seven bars)
soon modulates to D minor, closing in that key in
a manner similar to the first.   The third section
(ten bars) consists of modulation and slight development, and closes in A minor.   The fourth section
(fifteen bars) passes by means of broken chords
(in imitation of the last bar of the previous section)
through various keys, ending in the same fashion
as the first section, only, by way probably of in-
tensification at the end, there are seven instead of
four quaver chords ; the section, of course, ends
in F.   This movement in the matter of form offers
an interesting link between Kuhnau and E. Bach.
The second movement is a minuet, with variations ;
it certainly has a beginning, but seems endless.
The 3rd Sonata, in A, resembles No. 1 in form,
also in grouping of movements.

And in addition to the sonata of Mattheson, the Sei
Sonatine per Violino e Cembalo, di Georgio Philippo
Telemann, published at Amsterdam in 1721, will
give us an approximate idea of the clavier sonata
between Kuhnau and Emanuel Bach.   Each number,
by the way, is headed—title-page notwithstanding

—a sonata. No. 1, in A major, consists of four movements, Adagio, Allegro, Largo, Allegro, and all the four are in binary form. The second is naturally the most important; the others are very short and simple. In this Allegro, besides the allusion in the dominant key to the theme at the opening of the second section there is a return to it, after modulation, in the principal key. Some of the other sonatas are longer, but No. 1 represents, roughly, the other five as to form and contents. No. 6, in F, by the way, has only three movements: Vivace, Cantabile, and Presto.

The "Sonate per Gravicembalo, novamente composte," published by Giovanni Battista Pescetti in 1739, deserve notice, since they appeared three years before the six sonatas dedicated by Emanuel Bach to Frederick the Great. They are nine in number. In style of writing, order, and character of movements, they bear the stamp of the period in which they were written. Most of the movements in binary form are of the inter-mediate type, *i.e.* they have the principal theme in the dominant at the beginning of the exposition section, and again, later on, in the principal key. There is considerable variety in the order and number of movements. No. 1, for instance, has an Adagio, an Allegro, and a Menuett with variations. No. 2, in D, has four movements: Andante, Adagio, Allegro, Giga; the short Adagio is in D minor. No. 3, in G minor: Presto and A Tempo Giusto (a dignified fugue).

The influence of Handel is strong, also that of Scarlatti. Bars such as the following—

 etc.

foreshadow, in a curious manner, the *Alberti* bass.

A great number of clavier sonatas were written about the time during which Emanuel Bach flourished: his first sonatas appeared in 1742, his last in 1787. An interesting collection of no less than seventy-two sonatas (sixty-seven by various composers; five anonymous), issued in twelve parts, under the title *Oeuvres mêlées* (twelve books, each containing six sonatas), was published by Haffner at Würzburg, somewhere between 1760 and 1767. And another collection of symphonies and sonatas, principally by Saxon composers, was published at Leipzig in 1762 under the title *Musikalisches Magazin*. We will give the names of some of the chief composers, with titles of their works, adding a few other details. It is difficult in some cases to ascertain the year of publication; and it is practically impossible to say when the sonatas were actually composed :—

BACH, Wilh. Friedemann. Sei sonate, No. 1,[1] D major (Dresden, 1745). Sonata in C (published in Litolff's *Maîtres du Clavecin*), and others in D and G (autographs), and in F, A, and B flat (manuscripts).

BACH, Joh. Ernst. Two sonatas (in *Oeuvres mêlées*).

---

[1] The public did not support the undertaking, and the other five never appeared.

NICHELMANN, Christoph. Sei brevi sonate, etc., Op. 2 ;
Nuremberg (between 1745–1756).

HASSE. Two sonatas in E flat and B flat (manuscript ;
on one is the date of 1754). Two sonatas, one in D
minor (only one Lento movement) ; the other in D
major (only one Allegro movement in old binary form).
These are both in the Leipzig collection named above.

BENDA, Georg. Sei sonate (Berlin, 1757). Sonatas in
G, C minor, and G, also seven sonatinas (Vermischte
Clavierstücke, Gotha, 1780).

WAGENSEIL, Georg. Sonata (*Oeuvres mêlées*). Six sonatas
for the harpsichord (with accompaniment for a violin).[1]
Opera prima. (A. Hummel, London.)

SCHAFFRATH, Christoph.[2] Six sonates, Op. 2 (published
by Haffner, Nuremberg, 1754).

MOZART, Leopold. Three sonatas (*Oeuvres mêlées*).

MÜTHEL, Joh. Gottfr. Three sonatas, etc. (Haffner,
Nuremberg, about 1753) ; three sonatas (autograph).

UMSTATT, Joseph.[3] One sonata (*Oeuvres mêlées*). Sonata
consisting of only a Minuetto, Trio, and Gigue (Leipzig
collection). And the two Italians—

GALUPPI. Sonate per cembalo (London) ; and

PARADIES, P. Domenico. Twelve sonate di gravicembalo
(London).

GRÉTRY, Belgian composer (1741–1813), wrote "Six
sonates pour le clavecin" (1768), to which, unfortunately, we have not been able to gain access.

---

[1] The copy in the British Museum has no violin part, which was
probably unimportant.

[2] Emanuel Bach's predecessor as clavecinist at the Prussian
Court.

[3] This name is not in Mendel, Riemann, Grove, nor Brown.
Fétis, however, mentions him as Joseph Umstadt, *maître de chapelle*
of Count Brühl, at Dresden, about the middle of the eighteenth
century, and as composer of *Parthien*, and of six sonatas for the
clavecin.

From the two collections, etc., may be gathered many facts of interest. First, as regards the number and character of movements in a sonata. Emanuel Bach kept, for the most part, to three : two fast movements, divided by a slow one.[1]   In the second of his Leipzig collections (1780), there are two with only two movements (Nos. 2 and 3 ; a few bars connecting the two movements of No. 3). But among other composers there are many examples ; in some sonatas, the first movement is a slow one; in others, both movements are quick, in which case the second one is frequently a minuet.[2]   All twelve sonatas of Paradies have only two movements.

Of sonatas in three movements, some commence with a slow movement followed by two quick movements.[3]   (In one instance, in E Bach's sonatas, the 1st Collection, No. 2, in F, we even find two slow movements followed by a quick one, Andante, Larghetto, Allegro assai.) But the greater number had the usual order :— Allegro or Allegretto, Andante or Adagio, and Allegro or Presto.   Thus Hasse, Nichelmann, Benda, and other composers.   Now in E. Bach's Würtem-

---

[1] See, however, the early Würtemberg sonatas.

[2] Examples to be found in Rolle, Müthel, and Joh. Chr. Bach, etc.

[3] Gluck's six sonatas for two violins and a thorough bass, published by J. Simpson, London (probably about the time when Gluck was in London, since he is named on title-page "Composer to the Opera"), have three movements : slow, fast, fast,—the last generally a Minuet.

berg sonatas we found all three movements were in the same key, and there are similar cases in Hasse, Fried. Bach, Joh. Ernst Bach, etc.; but for the most part, the middle (slow) movement was in some nearly related key; in a sonata commencing in major—in the relative, or tonic minor, or minor under - dominant; and even (as in a sonata by Adlgasser) in the upper - dominant. Joh. C. F. Bach, in one instance, selected the minor key of the upper-dominant, and there are examples of more remote keys (E. Bach, Coll. of 1780, No. 1). With sonatas commencing in minor, the key selected for the middle movement was generally the relative major of the under-dominant, or that of the tonic; sometimes even tonic major. A very extraordinary example of a remote key is to be met with in Bach's Collection of 1779, No. 3 : his opening movement is B minor, but his middle one, G minor.[1]

It should be mentioned with regard to sonatas in three movements commencing in a minor key, that the last generally (in works of this period) remains and ends in minor. In modern sonatas the major is often found, at any rate before the close (see Beethoven, Op. 10, No. 1, etc.).

Baldassare Galuppi, born in 1706 on the island of Burano, near Venice, was a pupil of Lotti's.

---

[1] E. Bach did some strange things. One of his sonatas (Coll. of 1783, No. 1) has the first movement in G major, the second in G minor, and the third in E major.

Two sets of six " Sonate per il cembalo " of his were published in London. We cannot give the date, but may state that a sonata of his in manuscript bears the date 1754 (whether of copy or composition is uncertain ; anyhow, the year given acts as limit). The variety in the number of the movements of the published sonatas (one has four, some have three, some two, while No. 2 of the first set has only one) points to a period of transition. This alone, apart from the freshness and charm of the music, entitles them to notice. Much of the writing is thin (only two parts), and, technically, the music far less interesting than the Scarlatti pieces. Some of the phrases and figures, and the occasional employment of the Alberti bass, tell, however, of the new era soon about to be inaugurated by Haydn. There is one little feature in the 1st Sonata of the first set which may be mentioned. In the second section of the Adagio (a movement in binary form) of that sonata, the theme appears, as usual then, at the beginning of the second section, and, later on, reappears in the principal key, but it starts on the fourth, instead of the eighth quaver of the bar.

There was great variety in the order of movements. Sometimes a slow movement was followed by two quick movements ;[1] and the third movement was frequently a minuet. The quick movement sometimes came in the middle (Galuppi, Sonata in

[1] Galuppi, No. 4, first set : Adagio, Spiritoso, Giga Allegro.

B flat), sometimes at the beginning (E. Bach,
Coll. 1781, No. 3), sometimes at the end (E.
Bach, Coll. 1779, No. 2). Then, again, sometimes all, but frequently two of the three movements, were connected, *i.e.* the one passed to the
other without break.

So much for sonatas in two or three movements. But among the *Oeuvres mêlées* there
are no less than twenty which have four movements — some in the old order: slow, fast,
slow, fast; others in a new order: Allegro,
Andante or Adagio, Minuet, and Allegro or
Presto.[1] Thus Wagenseil[2], Houpfeld, J. E.
Bach, Hengsberger, and Kehl. Sometimes (as in
Seyfert and Goldberg) the Minuet came immediately after the Allegro[3] (see Beethoven chapter
with regard to position of Minuet or Scherzo in
his sonatas). In a sonata by Schaffrath, the
opening Allegro is followed by a Fugue. Again
(in Spitz, Zach, and Fischer) the following order
is found: Allegro, Andante, Allegro, Minuet.
In Fischer all the movements are in one key;
only the Trio of the Minuet is in the tonic minor.

[1] Sometimes the last movement was a Tempo di Menuetto, a
Polonaise, or even a Fugue.
[2] Wagenseil's Op. 1, Sonatas with violin accompaniment.
No. 4, in C, has Allegro, Minuetto, Andante, and Allegro assai.
[3] As this experiment of Seyfert and Goldberg, in connection with
Beethoven, is of special interest, we may add that Goldberg has
all the movements in the same key, but Seyfert has both the Trio
of the Minuet, and the Andante in the under-dominant. This
occurs in two of his sonatas; in both, the opening key is major.

In Spitz the Andante is in the under-dominant, the other movements being in the principal key. In Zach the Andante is in the minor tonic, and the third movement in the upper-dominant.   It is well to notice that *in none of these four-movement sonatas are the movements connected.*   The same thing is to be observed in Beethoven, with exception, perhaps, of Op. 110.   In the *Oeuvres mêlées* there is only one instance of a sonata in *five* movements by Umstatt.   It consists of an Allegro, Adagio (in the dominant), Fugue Allegro (in the relative of dominant), a Minuet in the principal key, with Trio in relative minor ; and, finally, a Presto.   By way of contrast, we may recall the two sonatas of Hasse, in one movement, already mentioned, and also the last of Emanuel Bach's six sonatas of 1760.

The works of many of the composers named in connection with differences in the number and order of movements are forgotten ; and, in some cases, indeed, their names are not even thought worthy of a place in musical dictionaries. Yet these variations are of great moment in the history of development.   And this for a double reason.   First, many of the works must have been known to E. Bach, and yet he seems to have remained, up to the last, faithful to the three-movement plan.   One or two of his sonatas have only two movements, none, however, has four.   Secondly, the experiment of extending the number to more than three, practically passed unheeded by Dussek, Clementi, Mozart,[1] Haydn,[2] and by all the composers of importance until Beethoven. The last-named commenced with sonatas in four movements; but, as will be seen in a later chapter, he afterwards became partial to the scheme of three movements.

Let us now consider, and quite briefly, movements in binary form; again, in this matter, some instructive facts will be gathered from the works of Bach's contemporaries. As in Scarlatti, so here we find the first of the two sections into which such a movement is divided, ending in one case[3] in the tonic, but, as a rule, in the dominant. There is, however, an instance of the close in the under-dominant (Müthel, No. 2 of the Sonatas of 1780), and in E. Bach, in the relative minor of the under-dominant (Sonatas of 1780, No. 3, Finale). In a minor key, the first section closed either in

[1] There is, however, one curious exception. The first of the two "Sonates pour le clavecin, qui peuvent se jouer avec l'Accompagnement de Violon, dédiées à Madame Victoire de France, par J. G. Wolfgang Mozart de Salzbourg, agé de sept ans," published at Paris as Op. 1, has *four* movements : an Allegro in C (with, by the way, an Alberti bass from beginning to end, except at the minor chord with organ point near the close of each section, the place for the extemporised cadenza), an Andante in F (Alberti bass from beginning to end), a first and second Menuet, and an Allegro molto, of course, in C. The brief dedication to Op. 1 is signed :—"Votre très humble, très obéissant et très petit Serviteur, J. G. Wolfgang Mozart."

[2] There is one exception : a sonata in G major, one of his earliest. See chapter on Haydn and Mozart.

[3] Scheibe ; a return for the moment to a practice which was once of usual occurrence.

the key of the relative major, or that of the dominant minor [1]—much more frequently the former.

Now, in proportion as the second part of the
first section grew more definite, so also did the
approach to it.   Everyone knows the pause so
frequently to be found in Haydn and Mozart, on
the dominant of the dominant, *i.e.* if the key of
the piece were C—

It is instructive to compare the less formal
methods of approaching the new key in E. Bach
and his contemporary Paradies ; with them it was
generally by means of a half-close.   It must be
remembered that E. Bach frequently has a movement quite on Scarlatti lines, *i.e.* without a
definite second subject ; [2] also that the second
subject in Bach's time was, as a rule, of secondary
importance.   But, curiously, in the Finale of a
sonata written by Leopold Mozart (father of the
great genius), after a half cadence on the dominant
of the dominant, *tempo* and measure change (from
Presto two-four, to Andante three-four, the latter remaining until the end of the first section), and the
same occurs in the recapitulation section ; by this
means the second theme was made specially prom-

---

[1] Mention has been made in this chapter of a first section in a
minor piece of Scarlatti's ending in the *major* key of the dominant.

[2] In the Sonatas of 1781, for instance, the first movement of No.
2, in F, has a definite second subject, but that is scarcely the case
with the first movement of No. 3, in F minor.

inent. In a sonata of Scarlatti's, in D, commencing

there is a definite second subject in, by the way,
the minor key of the dominant, and it is divided
from the first by two bars in common time (a
descending scale and a shake on a semibreve).
And then again, in No. 12 of the " Libro de XII.
Sonatas Modernas para Clavicordio," the second
subject is divided from the first by two bars of
common time (the piece is in Scarlatti's favourite
measure,three-eight), an ascending scale and a shake.
There are clear examples of a second subject,
besides E. Bach, in Eberlin, Fleischer, J. C. Bach,
and J. C. F. Bach. Yet even in Haydn's sonatas
one cannot always speak of a second subject.
The further history of the development of the
contents of the second half of the first section
shows, as it were, a struggle between two ideals.
One was *kinship*, *i.e.* the endeavour to present the
secondary matter in strong relationship to the
opening one (the opening notes or bars of a real
second subject were, indeed, frequently the same,
allowance being made, of course, for difference of
key) ; the other was *contrast*, *i.e.* the endeavour to
obtain variety. Haydn was more affected by the
first ; Mozart by the second. In Beethoven the two
are happily combined. It is important to notice
the closing bars of many first sections of the period
of which we are speaking. For instance, in E.
Bach, the first movement of the sonata in each

of the Collections of 1781 and 1783 has a concluding theme (as in the sonata of Scarlatti, and
frequently evolved from the opening theme).
Though in the complementary key, it cannot
count as "the second subject." It appears after
the complementary key has been ushered in by
one cadence, and after having apparently run its
course, it has been wound up by another. Then,
again, the portion between the cadences just
mentioned is at times filled with a true theme, so
that the concluding one, like the cave of Abra-
ham's field of Machpelah, is in reality an
appendency. *Sometimes there are several*: the enlargement of the exposition section by Beethoven,
and still more modern composers, so that it contains sometimes three, and even more themes, is
practically an exposition section on Scarlatti lines,
only on a larger scale: the figure has become a
phrase, mere connecting passages have acquired
organic meaning. The second section of Scarlatti's
movement in binary form contained a few bars of
development and modulation. Then a return
was made to the opening key of the piece, *but
never to the opening theme*; and in that key a
portion more or less great, more or less varied,
according to circumstances, was repeated. That
return to the opening theme is, as we have already
said, the landmark which divides binary from
sonata form.

In sonatas of the middle of the eighteenth century
the modulation section (in a major key) ended in

various ways,—on the dominant chord (of the principal key), on the tonic chord of the relative minor, the under-dominant, or even on the tonic itself of the principal key. Later on, Haydn and Mozart kept, for the most part, to the dominant chord. Beethoven, on account of the distant, and often abrupt, modulations of his middle sections, generally marked the approach to the recapitulation by clear, and often prolonged, dominant harmony; sometimes, however, the return of the principal theme comes as a surprise. The recapitulation always remained more or less faithful to the exposition. It is interesting to note how little the character and contents of the recapitulation section have been affected in modern times by the growth of the development section. In the matter of balance the two sections of movements in binary form are more satisfactory than the two sections (two, so far as outward division is concerned) of modern sonatas. The grain of mustard-seed in the parable grew into a tree, and so, likewise, have the few bars of modulation of early days grown into an important section. However difficult to determine the exact moment at which a movement in sonata-form really ceased to be binary, there seems no doubt that that moment has now passed. We have already noted when the change commenced.

CHAPTER II

JOHANN KUHNAU

THIS remarkable musician was born, April 1660,[1] at Geysing, where his grandfather, who, on account of his religious opinions, had been forced to leave Bohemia, had settled. Already in his ninth year young Kuhnau showed gifts for science and art. He had a pleasing voice, and first studied under Salomon Krügner, and afterwards under Christian Kittel,[2] organist of the Elector at Dresden. His next teachers were his brother Andreas Kuhnau, Alexander Hering,[3] and Vin-

[1] This is the date given by Mattheson. In some dictionaries we find 1667 ; this, however, seems to be an error, for that would only make Kuhnau fifteen years of age when he became candidate for the post of organist of St. Thomas'. Fétis, who gives the later date (1667), states that in 1684 Kuhnau became organist of St. Thomas', but adds : " Quoiqu'il ne fût agé que de dix-sept ans."

[2] This Kittel must surely have been father or uncle of Johann Christian Kittel, Bach's last pupil.

[3] Mattheson, in his *Grundlage einer Ehren-Pforte*, published at Hamburg in 1740, complains that the names of Salomon Krügner, Christian Kittel, A. Kuhnau, and Hering are not to be found in the musical dictionaries. The first and third have not, even now, a place.

cenzo Albrici. In 1680 the plague broke out at
Dresden, and Kuhnau returned to his parents.
He then went to Zittau with a certain Erhard
Titius, who had been *Praefectus* at the Kreuz-
schule, Dresden, and received help from the
court organist, Moritz Edelmann, also from the
"celebrated" Weise. A motet of Kuhnau's was
given at Zittau under his direction. After the
death of Titius, Kuhnau resided for a time in the
house of J. J. von Hartig, judge at Zittau. In 1682
he went to Leipzig, where D. Scherzer endeavoured
to obtain for him the post of organist at St.
Thomas'; Kühnel, however, was appointed. The
latter died in 1684, and was succeeded by Kuhnau,
who in 1700 also became cantor of St. Thomas'.
He devoted much of his time to jurisprudence.
Among other things, he wrote a curious satire,
entitled *Der musikalische Quacksalber*, published
in 1700. There remain in manuscript, *Tractatus
de tetrachordo* and *Introductio ad compositionem
musicalem.* Kuhnau had many pupils; we know
of two who afterwards became distinguished men.
The one was Christoph Graupner (1683–1760),
who in 1710 became capellmeister at Darmstadt.
In 1722, on the death of Kuhnau, Graupner,[1]

[1] In a letter written by Graupner to Mattheson, the former, after
mentioning that he studied the clavier and also composition under
Kuhnau, says:—"Weil ich mich auch bei Kuhnau, als Notist, von
selbsten ambot, u. eine gute Zeit für ihn schrieb, gab nur solches
gewünschte Gelegenheit, viel gutes zu sehen, u. wo etwa ein Zweifel
enstund, um mündlichen Bericht zu bitten, wie dieses oder jenes
zu verstehen?" (" As I offered myself as copyist to Kuhnau, and

who had been prize scholar under him, presented his testimonials, was examined, and seemed likely to become cantor as his teacher's successor. Meanwhile, however, John Sebastian Bach offered himself as candidate, and as Dr. Pepusch before Handel at Cannons in 1710, so did Graupner retire before his great rival. Mattheson, in his *Ehren-Pforte* (p. 410), tells us that " as a composer for the clavier, Graupner may rank as one of the best of his time." He wrote suites and sonatas for clavier. Johann Friedrich Fasch (1688–1758 or 9), the second pupil, soon after leaving Leipzig, where he had enjoyed Kuhnau's instruction from 1701–7, went to Italy, and on his return studied for a short time with Graupner. Fasch then filled various posts, until in 1722 (the very year indeed of Kuhnau's death) he became capellmeister at Anhalt Zerbst, where he remained until his death. His son, Carl Friedrich Christian, was the founder of the Berlin *Singakademie.* In 1756 Emanuel Bach had something to do with Fasch's appointment as clavecinist to Frederick the Great. The father, who was then seventy years of age, and who, like old Sebastian Bach, lived with the fear of God before his eyes, opposed the wish of his son to enter the service of the infidel king. Emanuel, who wished the younger Fasch to come to Berlin, wrote to the father to say " that in the

wrote some long time for him, such a wished-for opportunity enabled me to study much good (music), and, whenever a doubt arose to learn by word of mouth how this or that was to be understood.")

land over which Frederick the Great ruled, one could believe what one liked ; that the king himself was certainly not religious, but on that very account esteemed everyone alike." Bach offered to take young Fasch into his house, and to preserve him as much as possible from temptation. With regard to Graupner, it would be interesting to know whether in any of his sonatas (the autographs of which are, we believe, at Darmstadt) he worked at all on Kuhnau's lines. And with regard to Fasch, one would like to know whether he ever conversed with Emanuel Bach about his father, who taught him theory, and about Johann Kuhnau, his father's renowned teacher. It is from such by-paths of history that one sometimes learns more than from statements showing how son descended from sire, and how pupils were directly influenced by their teachers.

But it is as a musician that we are now concerned with Kuhnau, and, in the first place, as the composer of the earliest known sonata for the clavier. In 1695 he published at Leipzig—

" Sieben Partien aus dem Re, Mi, Fa, oder Terzia minore eines jedweden Toni, benebenst einer *Sonata* aus dem B. Denen Liebhabern dieses Instrumenten zu gar besondern Vergnügen aufgesetzet." That is—

Seven Partitas based on the Re, Mi, Fa, or minor third of each mode, together with a Sonata in B flat, for the especial gratification of lovers of this instrument.

With respect to this sonata, Kuhnau remarks in his preface: " I have added at the end a Sonata in B flat, which will please amateurs; for why should not such things be attempted on the clavier as well as on other instruments?" In such modest fashion was ushered into the world the first sonata for clavier, or, at any rate, the earliest with which we are acquainted.[1]

Mattheson, in *Das neu eröffnete Orchester* (1713), speaks about the *revival* of clavier sonatas, so that it is not quite certain whether that B flat Sonata was actually the first.[2] During the seventeenth century, sonatas were written for various instruments, with a figured bass for the cembalo.

It will, of course, be interesting to trace the influences acting upon Kuhnau. They were of two kinds: the one, Italian; the other, German. Corelli deserves first mention; and next, the Italian organist and composer, Vincenzo Albrici,[3] capellmeister to the Elector of Saxony from 1664–88, and afterwards organist of St. Thomas', Leipzig, who is known to have encouraged Kuhnau when young, and to have helped him to learn the Italian language. But German influence must also have been strong. Of Froberger special mention will be made later on. There was one

[1] In the *Dictionnaire de Musique* by Bossard (2nd ed. 1705) no mention is made under the article "Sonata" of one for the clavier, and yet the above had been published ten years previously.

[2] See also next chapter.

[3] Nearly the whole of this composer's works are said to have been destroyed at the bombardment of Dresden in 1760.

man, Diderich Becker, who published sonatas for
violins and bass already in 1668, and these, if we
mistake not, must have been well known to
Kuhnau. Apart from the character of the music,
the title of the work, *Musikalische Frülings
Früchte*, and the religious style of the preface,
remind one of Kuhnau's " Frische Früchte," also
of his preface to the "Bible" Sonatas. It is curious
to find the quaint expression " unintelligent birds "
used first by Becker, and afterwards by Kuhnau.

Let us describe briefly the above-mentioned B
flat Sonata. The first movement is in common
time, but the composer gave it no heading. It
is generally supposed (Becker, Rimbault, Pauer)
to be an Allegro; *moderato* might well be added,
for the stately, Handelian-like (the anachronism
must be excused) music will scarcely bear a rapid
tempo. The movement opens with an eight-bar
phrase, closing on the dominant. Then the music,
evolved from previous material, passes rapidly
through various related keys. After this modulation section there is a cadence to F major, and
in this, the dominant key, something like a new
subject appears, though it is closely allied to the
first. A return is soon made to the principal
key, but there is no repetition of the opening
theme. After a cadence ending on the tonic
(B flat), and two coda-like bars, comes a fugal
movement, still in the same key. The vigorous
subject, the well-contrasted counterpoint, the interesting episodes, and many attractive details

help one to forget the monotony of key so prevalent in the days in which this sonata was written. This, and indeed other fugues of Kuhnau show strong foreshadowings of Handel and Bach; of this matter, however, more anon. The counterpoint to the third entry of the subject is evolved from the opening subject of the sonata. The third movement consists of a fine Adagio in E flat, in the key of the subdominant and in three-four time. Then follows a short Allegro in three-four time, of polyphonic character. At the close of the movement Kuhnau has written the opening chords of the first movement with the words *Da Capo*. A similar indication is to be found in one of the "Frische Früchte" Sonatas. This repetition, also the third movement leading directly to the fourth, and the thematic connection mentioned above, would seem to show that the composer regarded the various sections of his sonata as parts of a whole.

In addition, Kuhnau wrote thirteen sonatas. The "Frische Clavier Früchte," or "Sieben Suonaten von guter Invention u. Manier auf dem Clavier zu spielen," were published in 1696, and later editions in 1710 and 1724. In a quaint preface the composer tells us that in naming his "Fresh Fruits" "sonatas," he kept in mind all kinds of *inventiones* and changes (Veränderungen) by which so-called sonatas are superior to mere partitas. Already a century before this preface was written, Praetorius had distinguished between two classes of instrumental music: the one, grave;

the other, gay. The composer has also a word to say about the graces or ornaments, the " sugar which sweetens the fruits." In modern reprints of Kuhnau the sugar is sometimes forgotten.[1] These " Frische Früchte " were followed by six " Bible " Sonatas in 1700. The former, both as regards form and contents, are remarkable. Kuhnau was a man of deeper thought and loftier conception than Emanuel Bach, but he was fettered by fugal forms,[2] and was fighting against them much in the same spirit in which Beethoven, a century later, fought against sonata-form, in the most general sense of that term. Beethoven was not only the more gifted, but he profited by the experiments of his predecessors, and he enjoyed the advantage of a vastly improved technique; Haydn, Mozart, Clementi, and others were the stepping-stones by which he rose to higher things. Kuhnau's attempts at sonata writing were bold, often rugged; and his experiments in programme-music, extraordinary. The latter were soon forgotten, while the clever, clear-formed sonatas of Emanuel Bach served as a gratification to the age in which he lived, and as guides to the composers who followed him. The "Frische Früchte," standing between Corelli and Emanuel Bach, are

---

[1] The sonata is given in *Le Trésor des Pianistes* with the ornaments, yet even there more than a dozen have been omitted.

[2] The clavier by its very nature tended towards polyphony; the violin towards monody. And, besides, Kuhnau prided himself on the fugal character of his sonatas.

skill in the workmanship which remind us of the
great Bach.   There are, indeed, resemblances to
Bach, also to Handel.   Scheibe, in his *Critischer
Musikus*, mentions Kuhnau, in conjunction with
Keiser, Telemann, and Handel, as one of the greatest
composers of the eighteenth century.   The mention
of Kuhnau together with Handel deserves note.
The constant discoveries which are being made of
Handel's indebtedness to other composers suggest
the thought that perhaps Kuhnau was also laid
under contribution.   No one, we think, can hear
the " Bible " Sonatas without coming to the conclusion that Handel was acquainted with the works
of his illustrious predecessor.   We will just place
side by side three passages from the " Bible "
Sonatas of Kuhnau with three from a harpsichord
suite of Handel—

"Bible" Sonata, No. 2.   KUHNAU.

Collection I., Suite 7, Ouverture.   HANDEL.

"Bible" Sonata, No. 6.   KUHNAU.

etc.

Collection I., Suite 7, Passacaille. HANDEL.

" Bible" Sonata, No. 6. KUHNAU.

Collection I., Suite 7, Passacaille. HANDEL.

It should be noticed that the three Handel
quotations are all from the same suite. We do
not mean to infer that the above passages from
Handel are plagiarisms, but merely that the
Kuhnau music was, unconsciously, in his mind
when he wrote them.

C. F. Becker, in his *Hausmusik in Deutschland*,
has suggested that these sonatas were known also
to Mozart, and begs us to look on this picture,
the opening of a Vivace movement in Kuhnau's
6th Sonata :—

and on this, from *The Magic Flute* :—

Faisst, however, justly observes that though the harmonic basis is the same in both, with Kuhnau the under-part is melody, whereas with Mozart it is the reverse. He also accuses Becker—and justly, as readers may see by turning to the passage in the *Zauberflöte*—of not having represented the passage quite honestly. Reminiscence hunters need to be very careful.

In these sonatas, as compared with the one in B flat, the thematic material is of greater importance ; and so, too, in the slow movements the writing is simpler and more melodious.

The rapid rate at which they were composed deserves mention. Kuhnau seems to have had the ready pen of a Schubert. In the preface to these " Frische Früchte " he says : " I wrote these seven sonatas straight off, though attending at the same time to my duties (he was *juris practicus*, also organist of St. Thomas'), so that each day one was completed. Thus, this work, which I commenced on the Monday of one week, was brought to an end by the Monday of the following week."

Kuhnau's second (and, so far as we know, last) set of sonatas bears the following title :—

Musikalische Vorstellung
Einiger
Biblischer Historien
In 6 Sonaten
Auf dem Klavier zu spielen
Allen Liebhabern zum Vergnügen
Verfüget
von
Johann Kuhnauen.

That is—

Musical Representation
of some
Bible Stories
In 6 Sonatas
To be performed on the Clavier
For the gratification of amateurs
Arranged
by
Johann Kuhnau.

Kuhnau was not the originator of programme-music. In the so-called *Queen Elizabeth Virginal Book*,[1] in the Fitzwilliam Library, there is a Fantasia by John Munday, who died 1630, in which there is given a description of weather both fair and foul. Again, Froberger, who died in 1667, is said to have been able, *on the clavier*, to describe incidents, ideas, and feelings; there is, indeed, in existence a battle-piece of his. And then Buxtehude (*d.* 1707) wrote a set of seven Suites for clavier, in which he is said to have represented

---

[1] Cf. *The Fitzwilliam Virginal Book*, edited by J. A Fuller-Maitland and W. Barclay Squire (Breitkopf & Härtel).

the nature and characteristics of the planets; these are, unfortunately, lost.   With Froberger's music, at any rate, Kuhnau was familiar.   In a long preface to these Bible stories, the composer refers to the subject of programme-music.   He reminds us how from ancient times musicians have tried to rival the masters of rhetoric, sculpture, and painting in terms of their own art.   And he expressly refers to programme pieces, and even to sonatas by the "distinguished Froberger[1] and other excellent composers."   The essence of his long, elaborate, and, at times, somewhat confused argument (it must be remembered that he was discussing a very difficult subject; and, also, that he was the first to write about it) is as follows :— He believes music capable by itself of producing wonderful effects, but in special cases, requiring the assistance of words.   Music, he tells us, can express sadness or joy; for that no words are necessary.   When, however, some individual—as in his sonatas—is referred to, words become essential, *i.e.* if one is to distinguish between the lamentation of a sad Hezekiah, a weeping Peter, or a mourning Jeremiah.   In other language, words are necessary to render the emotion definite.   Kuhnau gives a quaint illustration of the absolute necessity of words in certain cases; and that illustration is of particular interest, inasmuch as it points to still earlier, and possibly, clavier sonatas.   "I remember," says our author, "hearing a few years

[1] Johann Jakob Froberger died in 1667.

ago a sonata composed by a celebrated Chur-Fürst capellmeister, to which he had given the title, 'La Medica.' After—so far as I can recall —describing the whines of the patient and of his relations, the running of the latter to the doctor, the pouring forth of their sorrow, there came, finally, a Gigue, under which stood the words, 'The patient is progressing favourably, but has not quite recovered his health.' At this some mocked, and were of opinion that, had it been in his power, the author might well have depicted the joy at a perfect recovery. So far, however, as I could judge, there was good reason for adding words to the music. The sonata commenced in D minor; in the Gigue there was constant modulation towards G minor. At the final close, in D, the ear was not satisfied, and expected the closing cadence in G." In this wise was the partial recovery expressed in tones, and explained in words.

Except for the unmistakable seriousness of the author, this description might be taken as a joke, just as in one of the " Bible " Sonatas the deceit of Jacob is expressed by a deceptive cadence; but such extreme examples serve to emphasise the author's declaration that, at times, words are indispensable. Before noticing the sonatas themselves, one more quotation in reference to the same subject must be made from this interesting preface. The humblest scholar, Kuhnau tells us, knows the rule forbidding consecutive perfect consonances, and he speaks of certain strict *censores* who expose the clumsiness of *musical poets* who have refused to be bound by that rule. " But," says Kuhnau, in lawyer-like language : " *Cessante ratione prohibitionis cessat ipsa prohibitio.*" The term *musical poets* (the italics are ours) is a remarkable one; Kuhnau himself, of course, was one of them.

Philipp Spitta, in his *Life of J. S. Bach*, devotes one short paragraph to the Bible stories, and gives one or two brief quotations from the second; but they certainly deserve a longer notice.

The 1st Sonata is entitled " The Fight between David and Goliath." It opens with a bold section, intended, as we learn from a superscription, to represent *the bravado of Goliath*. The giant's characteristic theme, on which the whole section is built, is as follows :—

Then follows a section in A minor. A Chorale represents the prayer to God of the terrified Israelites, while the palpitating quaver accompaniment stands for the terror which seized them at sight of the giant; the harmonies are very striking. This Chorale setting should be compared with one by Bach (Spitta's *Life of Bach*, English edition, vol. i. p. 216), said to owe its existence to the influence of Georg Böhm, organist at Lüneburg at the commencement of the eighteenth century. Next comes a little pastoral movement (C major, three-

four time) expressive of David's courage and of his
confidence in God. Then a tone-picture is given
of the encounter; the heavy tread of the Philistine
is heard in the bass, while semiquaver passages,
evolved from a figure in the preceding movement,
evidently portray the spirited youth. One
realistic bar scarcely needs the explanation given
by Kuhnau that it is the slinging of the stone
which smote the Philistine in his forehead; and
the same may be said of the " Goliath falls " in
the following bar :—

Il combáttere frà l'uno e l'altro, e la loro contésa.

Vien tirata la selce colla frombola nella fronte del gigante

casca Goliath.

This section, limited to sixteen bars, is not only an early, but a notable specimen of programme-music; it is realistic, but not in the least ridiculous. Rapid passages with points of imitation tell of the flight of the Philistines. A bright movement (still in C) bears the superscription, "The joy of the Israelites at their victory"; in it there is an allusion to the pastoral movement. Maidens then advance, with timbrels and instruments of music, to meet the victor, and the sonata concludes with

a stately Minuet, similar in character to the
Minuet in the Overture to Handel's *Samson*; the
people are dancing and singing for joy.

The 2nd Sonata presents to us a very different
picture. Here we have the melancholy of Saul
driven away by means of music. There are a few
realistic effects, such as the paroxysms of madness
of Saul, and the casting of the javelin; but the
subject is one which readily lends itself to real
musical treatment. The music of the 1st Sonata
was principally objective; here, however, it is
principally subjective. In the first part of the
work the music depicts, now the sadness, now
the rage of the monarch. The opening is worthy
of Bach, and presents, indeed, a foreshadowing of
the opening of the 16th Prelude of the "Well-
tempered Clavier." Spitta mentions the fine fugue,
with the subject standing for the melancholy, the
counter-subject for the madness of the king; and
he justly remarks that these two images of Saul
"contain the poetical germ of a truly musical
development." The "dimly brooding" theme of
the fugue brings to one's mind the "Kyrie eleison"
fugue of Mozart's *Requiem*; also the theme of the
Allegro of Beethoven's Sonata in C minor (Op.
111), notwithstanding the fact that Kuhnau's is
slow and sad, but Beethoven's, fast and fiery.
Here is the first half of the former—

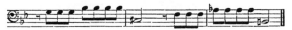

Let not our readers be deceived by the word

" fugue." The movement is no mere formal
scholastic piece of writing such as one might
expect; the preluding of David on his harp, the
" javelin " episode, the paroxysms of rage give to
it rather the character of a free fantasia. One
word with regard to the paroxysm passages. We
quoted above a sentence from the preface respecting the violation of the rule respecting consecutive
consonances by certain "poet musicians." Kuhnau,
under this plural mask, was, as we have mentioned,
certainly referring to himself, for in another part
of the preface he specially calls attention to
the consecutive fifths by which he depicts the
disordered mind of King Saul. This first movement, opening in G minor, ends on the chord
of G major. We now come to a movement
(B flat) entitled " The Refreshing Melody from
David's Harp." The following is part of David's
soothing theme :—

At first it is not heard in its entirety. The sweet
singer of Israel plays it, or sometimes only the
first two bars, in various keys, and with varied
harmonisation, as if watching the king and trying
the effect on him of different modulations. Besides in the principal key, it appears several times,
and in succession, in the relative minor, then in the

minor key of the supertonic. The key of the subdominant enters with refreshing effect; after that, a return is made to the principal key, which continues until the close of the movement. Between each delivery of the theme, occur passages similar to the following :—

as if to denote the restlessness of the king. And as the character of the music, especially towards the close, suggests *piano* and *pianissimo*, it would seem as though intended to express the gradual healing power of the music. As a piece of abstract music, the movement appears long, but not if the dramatic situation be kept well in mind. At length the sounds of the harp cease, and a closing, peaceful, and dignified movement in G minor tells of Saul's now tranquil state of mind.

The 3rd Sonata, entitled "The Marriage of Jacob," opens with a delightful Gigue; over it stands the superscription, "The joy of the family of Laban at the arrival of their relation Jacob." The beginning of the second section has, as usual, the subject inverted. The music is gay and sparkling. Then comes a section illustrative of Jacob's seven years' service for a wife. The music expresses effort and fatigue, but by way of musical contrast sprightly bars intervene from time to time, to represent happy moments when the lovers meet. Further on we have the bridal-song of the

companions of Rachel : a short, quaint, and delicate
movement in minor and in triple time.   It commences thus :—

A short section follows, full of rapid semiquaver
passages and points of imitation (such a mode of
procedure is frequently adopted by the composer) ;
and then comes a sudden change in the character
of the music.   No *tempo* is marked, but, evidently,
it must not be rapid.   It is a tone-picture of the
deception practised by Laban upon Jacob when
he substituted Leah in place of Rachel.   At first,
it is a free recitative.   A quotation of a few bars
will give a good idea of the extraordinary harmonies and rhythmical figures :—

And again—

The Fugue, short and vigorous, has a characteristic
theme :—

A new section expresses Jacob's happiness until
he discovers the deceit practised on him.   The

exact moment of displeasure is indicated by a superscription; the latter, however, was scarcely necessary—the notes speak for themselves. For there are reminiscences of the Laban recitative, of the fugue theme, and also (in augmentation) of the counter-subject. This is, indeed, an early instance of the employment of representative themes. The composer then naïvely orders the section descriptive of the wedding festivities to be repeated, to illustrate the second marriage of Jacob with the beloved Rachel.

The 4th Sonata deals with Hezekiah's mortal sickness and recovery. It is shorter than the preceding ones, and of simpler structure. It opens with slow, sad music: the prophet of God has summoned the king to prepare for death. His ardent prayer to heaven is naturally expressed by a well-known Chorale, supported by most effective polyphonic harmony. After a short thematic working of a figure from the Chorale, the latter is submitted to fresh treatment: the movement (in six-four time) somewhat resembles the old Corrente. The sonata concludes with a lively movement in binary form. It is intended to depict the king's joy at his recovery. There are a few bars *adagio* in each section: Hezekiah recalls the past. This is the only one of the sonatas which, as abstract music, would be satisfactory without any programme.

No. 5 is entitled " Gideon, the Saviour of Israel." From a musical point of view it is the least interesting of the set, yet it contains some

curious programme effects. It will be remembered
that a sign from heaven was given to Gideon : the
fleece was to be covered with dew, but the ground
to remain dry ; the next night, however, the order of
things was reversed. Kuhnau expresses the latter
by giving a theme in *contrary motion.* This may
almost be described as punning in music. The
composer, however, meant it seriously ; from the
tone of his preface, and the narration, with com-
ments, which he has prefixed to each sonata, in
addition to the explanatory words over the music
itself, it is clear that his aim was to elucidate and
intensify the Bible stories by means of his art.
He was a man, apparently, of deep religious belief.

The battle-picture is a curiosity, but, as music,
of little value. The flight of the Midianites is
depicted in the following primitive manner :—

The 6th (and last) Sonata bears the title, " The
Tomb of Jacob." We have, at first, mournful
music : the sons of the Patriarch are standing round
the deathbed. At length Jacob dies, and they
" ponder over the consequences of the sad event."
A quiet, expressive theme

is then treated fugally, and with marked effect
Then comes the journey from Egypt to the land
of Canaan. The bass, progressing in quavers,
expresses motion. From time to time a curious
syncopated semiquaver figure is heard in the
upper part: it may be intended to represent
sobbing. The following quotation, including one
of these " sobbing " passages, will give a good idea
of the character of this section—

A short, solemn phrase is headed, " The Burial of
Israel." Then a finely worked-out fugal section
depicts the great grief of the bystanders. It is in
four parts, but in one place the addition of a fifth
part and stretto treatment render the feeling of
grief more intense. A peaceful closing section in
the major key and in triple time expresses the
consoled minds of the survivors.

From this *résumé* of these " Bible " Sonatas, it will
be seen that they have nothing in common with
the ordinary sonata of the time in which they

were written. They were bold attempts at programme-music; and, as we have already said, the
form is entirely determined by the subject-matter.

In the old edition of these "Bible" Sonatas, in
addition to the preface of which we have made
mention, Kuhnau has related the Bible stories in
his own characteristic language. We give a trans-
lation of the first two, as specimens.

I. *The Combat between David and Goliath*

The portrait given in Scripture of great Goliath
is something quite uncommon: a monster of
nature appears, a giant, tall as a tree. Six ells
will not suffice to measure his length; the high
helmet of brass which he wears on his head makes
him appear still taller; and the scaly coat of mail,
the greaves of brass placed about his legs, together
with the enormously heavy shield which he carries,
also his strong spear, tipped with iron, like unto
a weaver's beam, sufficiently show that he is of
mighty strength, and that all these exceedingly
heavy loads do not inconvenience him in the
slightest. If the mere description of this man
creates fear, how much greater will not the terror
of the poor Israelites be when the living image
of this their enemy appears before them. For
he stands before them in his brazen armour,
rivalling the sun in brilliancy, makes with the
rustling of his armour a terrible din, and snorts
and bellows as if he would devour them at one

mouthful; his words sound in their ears like
dreadful thunder.   He holds in contempt his
enemies and their equipage, and demands that a
hero be sent out to him from their camp; this
combat is to show whose shoulders shall bear the
yoke of bondage.   By this means he imagines
that the sceptre will soon pass from the Israelites
to the Philistines.   But a miracle is about to
happen!   When courage fails all the heroes of
Israel, when the giant has only to show himself, to
cause them to flee, when, also, the terrible warrior
continues, according to his custom, to pour contempt on the enemy, David, a slim, courageous
stripling, a simple shepherd-boy, then appears, and
offers to fight the bully.   He is accused of rash-
ness.   This, however, troubles David but little; he
adheres firmly to his heroic resolution, and seeks
audience of King Saul.   By God's help, he had
fought with a bear and a lion who had taken from
him a lamb, had snatched the prey from the jaws
of these cruel beasts, and, further, had slain them.
Thus he hoped would end the struggle with this
bear and lion of a Philistine.   Strongly relying
upon God, he advances towards the powerful giant,
with a sling, and with some specially selected pebbles.
Then the Philistines think to themselves, " Now
will the great hero blow away the enemy like a
speck of dust, or kill him as he would a fly."   All
at once Goliath becomes terrible in his rage, and
raves, uttering frightful oaths at David, declaring
that he is treated as if he were a dog, and that

David comes to him with shepherd's staff, and not with weapons worthy of a warrior. David, however, is fearless. He relies on his God, and prophesies to the enemy that, though without sword, spear, or shield, he will cast Goliath to the ground; that he will cut off his head, and leave his carcase as food for birds and wild beasts. Hereupon David rushes at the Philistine, wounds him in the forehead with a sharp stone cast from his sling, so that Goliath falls to the ground. Before he has time to rise, David, making use of his opportunity, slays him with his own sword, and bears away from the field of battle, the hewn-off head as a trophy of victory. As formerly the Israelites fled before the snorting and stamping of the great Goliath, so now flee the Philistines in consequence of the victory of young David. Thus they give opportunity to the Israelites to pursue them, and to fill the roads with the corpses of the slain fugitives. It is easy to imagine how great must have been the joy of the victorious Hebrews. In proof of it, we learn how women came forth from the cities of Judea, with drum, fiddle, and other musical instruments, to meet the victors, and sang alternately: " Saul hath slain his thousands, but David his ten thousands."

Thus the sonata expresses—

1. The stamping and defying of Goliath.
2. The terror of the Israelites, and their prayer to God at sight of the terrible enemy.

3. The courage of David, his desire to humble the pride of the giant, and his childlike trust in God.

4. The contest of words between David and Goliath, and the contest itself, in which Goliath is wounded in the forehead by a stone, so that he falls to the ground and is slain.

5. The flight of the Philistines, and how they are pursued by the Israelites, and slain by the sword.

6. The exultation of the Israelites over their victory.

7. The praise of David, sung by the women in alternate choirs.

8. And, finally, the general joy, expressing itself in hearty dancing and leaping.

II. *David curing Saul by means of Music*

Among the heavy blows dealt to us at times by God, for holy reasons, are to be counted bodily sicknesses. Of these one can in a real sense say that they cause pain. Hence the invention of that physician of Padua was by no means ridiculous, who thus represented in picture-form, over his house-door, the various sicknesses: a man attacked by many dogs and gesticulating wildly, through pain. To each of these dogs was given a name, and each acted accordingly. The dog, Gout, was biting the man's foot; the dog, Pleurisy, his

loins; Stone, his kidneys; Colic, his belly, and so on.
Finally, a great sheep-dog, representing daily fever,
had thrown the man to the ground. The inventor
could easily have known (for that he did not
require any special experience) that sicknesses act
upon men in a manner not less gentle. By the
exercise of patience, pain can at length be con-
quered, although the soul, so intimately combined
with the body, must feel it not a little. But
when the soul is attacked by sickness, patience
always gives way; for bodily, cannot in any way
be compared with mental, suffering. Inner anguish
shows itself in restless gestures. Scripture takes
us into a lazaretto of such afflicted persons.
Among others, we meet with a royal and singular
patient. Saul is his name. Of him we read:
" The spirit of the Lord departed from Saul, and
he was vexed by an evil spirit from the Lord."
Where God is absent, and the Evil One present,
there must dwell all manner of evil. The
hateful aspect of this man in his paroxysms
of pain can readily be imagined. His eyes
turn the wrong way, and sparks of fire, so to
speak, dart out one after the other; his face is so
disfigured, that human features can scarce be
recognised; his heart casts forth, as it were, a
wild, stormy sea of foam. Distrust, jealousy,
envy, hatred, and fear burst forth from him.
Especially does the javelin, constantly flying from
his hand, show that his heart rages fiercely with
anger. To sum up: his soul-sickness is so great that

the marks of hellish tortures can be clearly traced. At lucid intervals (*lucidis intervallis*) or quiet hours, the tortured king realises his indescribable evil; and he therefore seeks after a man who can cure him.   But under such extraordinary circumstances can help be hoped for?   From human arts, Saul could not expect any salvation.   But God sometimes works wonders among men.   So he sends to him a noble musician, the excellent David, and puts uncommon power into his harp-playing.   For when Saul, so to speak, is sweating in the hot bath of sadness, and David plays only one little piece, the king is at once refreshed, and brought into a state of repose.

Thus the sonata represents—

1. Saul's sadness and madness.
2. David's refreshing harp-playing, and
3. Tranquillity restored to the king's mind.

CHAPTER III

IN the year 1637 was born at Massa de Valnevola
(Tuscany) Bernardo Pasquini,[1] who is said to have
been one of the most distinguished performers on
the organ and also the harpsichord. He studied
under Loreto Vittori and Antonio Cesti, but his
real master was evidently Palestrina, whose scores
young Bernardo studied with fervent zeal. He
was appointed organist of Santa Maria Maggiore,
Rome, and, according to the monument erected to
his memory by his nephew, Bernardo Ricordati,
and his pupil, Bernardo Gaffi, in the church of San
Lorenzo in Lucina of that city, the composer was
for a time in the service of Battista, Prince Borghese.
The inscription runs thus :—

"D. O. M.

" Bernardo Pasquino Hetrusco e Massa Vallis
Nevolæ Liberianæ Basilicæ S. P. Q. R. Organedo
viro probitate vitæ et moris lepore laudatissimo
qui Excell. Jo. Bap. Burghesii Sulmonensium
Principis clientela et munificentia honestatus

---

[1] Meyer thinks he was probably the son of Ercole Pasquini, born
about 1580, and predecessor of Frescobaldi at St. Peter's.

musicis modulis apud omnes fere Europæ Principes
nominis gloriam adeptus anno sal. MDCCX. die
XXII. Novembris S. Ceciliæ sacro ab Humanis
excessit ut cujus virtutes et studia prosecutus
fuerat in terris felicius imitaretur in coelis. Bernardus Gaffi discipulus et Bernardus Ricordati ex
sorore nepos præceptori et avunculo amantissimo
moerentes monumentum posuere. Vixit annos
LXXII. menses XI. dies XIV."

Pasquini enjoyed reputation as a dramatic composer, and the success of an opera of his performed
at the Teatro Capranica, Rome, during the festivities
in honour of Queen Christina of Sweden (1679),
is specially noted ; or, according to Mendel, he
wrote two successful operas, one for the opening
of the Teatro Capranica, and a second for the
festivals. He also wrote an oratorio : *La Sete di
Christo.* Pasquini died in the year 1710.

But, it will be asked, Why is he mentioned in
a book which is concerned with the sonata ? It
is known that he was a skilful performer on the
harpsichord, and some Toccatas and Suites of his
appear to have been published in a collection of
clavier music at Amsterdam in 1704. Fétis,
in his *Biographie Universelle des Musiciens,* even
states that he wrote sonatas for *gravicembalo.*
Here are his words :—

" Landsberg possédait un recueil manuscrit original de pièces d'orgue de Pasquini, dont j'ai extrait
deux toccates, composées en 1697. Ce manuscrit
est indiqué d'une manière inexacte dans le catalogue

de la bibliothèque de ce professeur (Berlin, 1859) de cette manière : Pasquini (Bernardo) *Sonate pei Gravicembalo* (libro prezioso). Volume grosso *E scritto di suo (sua) mano in questo libro.* Ce même catalogue indique aussi de Bernard Pasquini : *Saggi di contrapunto*—Anno 1695. Volume forte. *E scritto di suo (sua) mano in questo libro.* Malheureusement ces précieux ouvrages sont passés en Amérique avec toute la bibliothèque musicale du professeur Landsberg."

Whether these precious volumes actually went to America seems doubtful. Anyhow both volumes are now safely housed in the Berlin Royal Library. It may be mentioned that the first contains no real sonata : its contents consist principally of suites, toccatas, variations, and fugues.

In the story of Italian instrumental music, Pasquini is little more than a name. The fourth volume of A. W. Ambros' *History of Music* concludes thus :—" So ist uns von dem gerühmten Meister nichts geblieben, als seine Name u. seine stolze Grabschrift in San Lorenzo in Lucina." (Thus of the famous master (*i.e.* Pasquini) nothing remains except his name and his proud monument in San Lorenzo in Lucina). The writer of the article " D. Scarlatti," in Sir George Grove's *Dictionary of Music and Musicians*, remarks that the famous harpsichord player and composer " has been called a pupil of Bernardo Pasquini." But he considers this " most improbable, seeing that Pasquini was of the school of Palestrina, and wrote entirely in

the contrapuntal style, whereas Domenico Scarlatti's chief interest is that he was the first composer who studied the peculiar characteristics of
the free style of the harpsichord."

Of Pasquini as a performer on the harpsichord,
Mattheson relates " how on his visit to Rome he
found Corelli playing the violin, Pasquini the
harpsichord, and Gattani the lute, all in the
orchestra of the Opera-house."   And, once more,
in the notice of Pasquini in the same dictionary,
we are informed that the composer " exercised a
certain influence on German musicians."   In C.
F. Weitzmann's *Geschichte des Clavierspiels* there
is an interesting reference to some Toccatas of
Pasquini published in " Toccates et suites pour le
clavecin de MM. Pasquini, Paglietti et Gaspard
Kerle, Amsterdam, Roger, 1704."   A Toccata was
published (most probably one of those in the above
work) by I. Walsh in his

Second Collection
of
Toccates, Vollentarys and Fugues
made on purpose for the
Organ and Harpsichord
Compos'd by
Pasquini, Polietti
and others
The most Eminent Foreign Authors.

Of Polietti,[1] court organist at Vienna before J.

[1] Weitzmann and other writers, in referring to the work published
at Amsterdam, spell the name Paglietti ; it should, however, be
Polietti or Poglietti.

S. Bach was born, Emil Naumann has, by the way, given an interesting account in an article " Ein bisher unbekannt gebliebener Vorgänger Seb. Bach's unter den Italienern " (*Neue Berl. Mus.-Ztg.* Jahrgang 29). The Toccatas of Pasquini, published by Roger, and a so-called " Sonata," [1] printed by Weitzmann in the work just referred to, constitute, we believe, all that has hitherto appeared in print of this composer.

And yet surely Pasquini may lay claim to a place in the history of instrumental music and the sonata, for he not only wrote suites, but also sonatas for the harpsichord, or, to be quite exact, for two harpsichords. Some, at any rate, of his music is to be found in the British Museum. There are three volumes (Add. MSS. 31,501–3). On the fly-leaf of the first is written :—

" Ad Usum Bernardi Felicij Ricordati de Baggiano in Etruria."

Then comes in pencil a note probably made when the volumes came into the possession of the British Museum :—

" These are original MSS. by the hand of Bernardo Pasquini, 1637–1710, the greatest organist of Italy in the second half of the 17th century, and written for his nephew B. Ricordati. They are the only MSS. of Pasquini known to be

---

[1] This piece was printed from a manuscript in the British Museum, which bears no such title. Judging, however, from the title of the *libro prezioso* mentioned on p. 71, that name may originally have been given to it.

in Europe.   This vol. is dated at the end, Dec.
3, 1704 ; at the beginning, May 6, 1703."

And now for its contents.   The first piece
is a short suite,[1] consisting of a Tastata (the old
term for Prelude), a Corrente and an Aria ;
and it shows that Pasquini could write homo-
phonic as well as polyphonic music.   Then
follows a piece in the key of D major, headed

" A due Cembali, 1704, Bernardo Pasquini,"

which consists of three movements.   First one commencing with chords, after which, fugal imitation.
Next we have a fugal movement, like the preceding one, in common time ; lastly, one in six-eight
time.   All three movements are in the same key.
The part for each cembalo is written on a separate
stave, the one below the other.   Only the bass
notes are written, and the upper parts are indicated
by figures.   But this will be clearer presently, for
we shall give one or more illustrations.   At the
close of the six-eight movement is written *fine*,
and on the following page another piece begins
in C major, marked merely 2a, commencing
thus :—

This theme reminds one of Bach's Adagio from
the 2nd Organ Concerto—

---

[1] The suite is printed in the *Pasquini-Grieco Album* by Messrs.
Novello.

Clav. e Ped.

or even Handel's "Along the Monster Atheist
strode."[1] The movements of this second piece
are similar in structure and character to those of
the first. Next we have a piece of lighter character in two movements, and, apparently, for one
cembalo: there is, of course, only one bass part
(figured). At the commencement is merely
marked *Basso continuo*. The following piece is
headed 3a Sonata (3rd Sonata). It is in the
key of D minor, and it has three movements, all
in the same key. Now, as all the pieces for *two
cembali* in the volume after this are marked as
sonatas, coupled with the fact that before this
3rd Sonata there are two pieces for two cembali,
the latter of which is marked 2a (second),
we may conclude that these two are also sonatas.
The piece for one cembalo between the 2nd and
3rd Sonatas is, as we have remarked, of lighter
character, and was possibly considered a suite.
After the 3rd Sonata comes a fourth, then a *Basso
continuo* (containing, however, by exception, more

[1] Pasquini was no doubt one of the many composers who influenced
Handel. When the latter visited Italy before he came to London
in 1710, he made the acquaintance of the two Scarlattis (Alessandro
and Domenico), Corelli, and other famous musicians at Rome ; of
Lotti and Steffani at Venice ; and surely at Naples he must have
known Pasquini, whose name, however, is not to be found either in
Schoelcher or Rockstro. Only Gasparini, who was a pupil of
Pasquini's, is mentioned by the former.

than one suite), and so on, alternately, until the
14th Sonata is reached. Then follows the last
piece in the volume. The superscription, " For
one *or* two cembali," [1] leads us to believe that the
preceding *Basso continuo* numbers were intended
for one cembalo. It should be stated that movements in binary form are rare among the sonatas,
frequent among the *Basso continuo* pieces,—
another reason for considering the latter suites.

The structure of the 3rd Sonata [2] is extremely
simple. The first, probably an Allegro moderato,
opens with a bold characteristic phrase, which
is repeated in the second bar by the second
cembalo; points of imitation, in fact, continue
throughout the movement. At the seventh bar
there is modulation to the dominant, and at the
ninth, to the subdominant, in which the opening
theme recurs. A stately antiphonal passage leads
back to the principal key, and the movement
concludes with a cadence such as we find in many
a work of Bach's or Handel's. The Adagio opens
with short phrases for each instrument alternately.
A new subject in the relative major is treated in
imitative fashion. After a return to the opening
theme, also an allusion to the second theme, a new
figure is introduced, but the movement soon comes
to a close. This slow movement brings to one's
mind " The Lord is a Man of War," and the
major section of the duet, " Thou in Thy Mercy,"

---

[1] " Si puo fare a Due Cembali.
[2] See the *Novello Album*.

in Handel's *Israel in Egypt.*   The third movement,
in structure, much resembles the first; the music
is broad and vigorous.   The closing bars suggest
the stringendo passage and presto bars in the coda
of the Scherzo of the "Choral Symphony."   Of
course it is disappointing to have only the bass
parts for each instrument.   The volume, as we
have already stated, was for the use of Ricordati,
and probably the uncle and nephew performed
these sonatas together.   Musicians will be able
to write out the figured basses, and thus form
some idea of the music.   The figures are an outline of what was in the composer's mind; but these
basses, like those of Bach and Handel, so simple,
so clear to the composers who penned them, will
always remain more or less a *crux criticorum.*   It
will be noticed that the three movements, as in
some of Corelli's sonatas, are all in the same key.

We now give the opening bars of the three
movements of the piece for one or two cembali :—

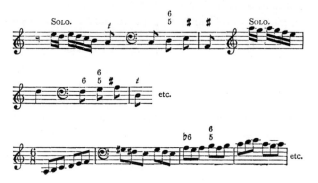

All the other sonatas are more or less after the pattern of the one given. The other two volumes contain suites, airs with variations, arias, and a quantity of short figured basses, apparently as studies.

Before closing this short chapter we will add a word or two about Italian music for the harpsichord at the beginning of the eighteenth century. A recent writer remarks that " Domenico Scarlatti seems to spring full-armed into the view of history." But his father, the renowned opera-writer, Alessandro Scarlatti, wrote music for the harpsichord, also his pupil, Gaëtano Grieco, who succeeded him as Professor at the Conservatoro dei poveri di Gesù Cristo (Naples) in 1717. The influence of the master can be clearly traced in the music of the pupil; and, if one may judge from the simpler character of Grieco's music [1] as compared with that of D. Scarlatti, he, too, was a predecessor. Grieco is said to have been born about 1680; D. Scarlatti was born in 1683; but this, of course, decides nothing as to the dates of their compositions. The harpsichord music of G. Grieco has both character and charm, and it is indeed strange that none of his pieces have been included either in the *Trésor des Pianistes*, the *Maîtres du Clavecin*, or Pauer's Collections of old music.

---

[1] See the *Novello Album*.

This chapter is headed : " A Contemporary of Kuhnau." The latter published all his known sonatas by the year 1700, while the dates assigned to the Pasquini sonata volume are, as we have seen, 1703–4. But at that time Pasquini was over sixty years of age ; it is therefore more than probable that he was really the predecessor of the German master as a writer of clavier sonatas.

CHAPTER IV

EMANUEL BACH AND SOME OF HIS
CONTEMPORARIES

CARL PHILIPP EMANUEL, third son of J. S. Bach,
was born at Weimar, 8th or 14th March, 1714,
and died at Hamburg, 14th December, 1788. He
studied composition and clavier-playing with his
father. His brother, Wilhelm Friedemann, his
senior by four years, went through a similar
course, but learnt, in addition, the violin under
J. G. Graun. Emanuel's attention, however, was
concentrated on the one instrument; and to this
we probably owe the numerous clavier sonatas
which he wrote, and which paved the way for
those of Haydn, Mozart, and Beethoven. In his
twenty-first year (1735) Emanuel left his father's
house in order to study jurisprudence at Frankfort-on-the-Oder; three years later, however, he
went to Berlin, and as cembalist entered the service
of Frederick the Great (1740).[1]   Already in

[1] The post was offered to Bach in 1738, while Frederick was as
yet Crown Prince, but he only entered on his duties in 1740.

his father's house, the young student saw and
heard many distinguished musicians; he himself
has told us that no musician of any note passed
through Leipzig without seeking an opportunity
to meet his father, so famed as composer and
as performer on the organ and clavier.   And
again, afterwards, at the Court of Prussia, he came
into contact with the most notable composers and
performers of his day.   From among these may
be singled out C. H. Graun (composer of the
"Tod Jesu") and Georg Benda.[1]   Graun was
already in the service of Frederick when the
latter was only Crown Prince.[2]   It would be
interesting to learn the special influences acting
upon Emanuel before he published his first set of
sonatas in 1742, but this is scarcely possible.
The collection of symphonies[3] or sonatas published at Leipzig in 1762, mentioned in our
introductory chapter, gives, however, some idea of

[1] The four sons of Hans Georg Benda (Franz, Johann, Georg,
and Joseph) were excellent musicians, and all members of the band
of Frederick the Great.   Georg, the third son, composer of *Ariadne*
and *Medea*, two *duodramas* which attracted the attention of Mozart,
was, however, the most remarkable.

[2] Cf. Carlyle's *Frederick the Great*, vol. iv. p. 134 :—"Graun,
one of the best judges living, is likewise off to Italy, gathering
singers."

[3] The symphonies appear to be three-movement overtures tran-
scribed for clavier.   As a rule, the pieces marked as symphonies in
this collection have no double bars, and, consequently, no repeat in
the first movement.   A "symphony" of Emanuel Bach is, however,
marked as a "sonata" in the *Six Lessons for the Harpsichord*,
published in London during the eighteenth century.

the music of that period; and it is possible that many of the numbers were written before Emanuel Bach published his first works. The "Sammlung Vermischte Clavierstücke für geübte und ungeübte Spieler," by Georg Benda, may also be mentioned; it is of great interest, especially the Sonata in C minor. The character of the music and style of writing for the instrument constantly remind one of Emanuel Bach. Benda, born in 1721, joined the King of Prussia's Band in 1742, and soon became known as an experienced performer on the harpsichord. Unfortunately it is impossible to ascertain the dates of composition of the various pieces of this collection, and thus to find out whether Benda was an imitator of Bach or *vice versâ*; the collection itself was only published at Gotha in 1780.

The Italian taste in music which prevailed at the Prussian Court[1] had undoubtedly a marked influence on Bach, and one for good. The severe counterpoint of the North German school and the suave melody of the Sunny South blended together with happy results.

It is customary to speak *en bloc* of Emanuel Bach's sonatas; if, however, the earlier be compared with some of the later ones, interesting differences may be detected, and developments

[1] The king was extremely fond of Hasse's music, but this composer, though German by birth, was thoroughly Italian by training.

traced. But the composer's artistic career, unfortunately, does not show a steady, regular advance such as we find in J. S. Bach or Beethoven. C. H. Bitter, his biographer and enthusiastic admirer, has to confess that he was a practical man, and that he wrote at times to please pupils and amateurs; while, occasionally, his aim may have been pecuniary gain.

Of his early period, we shall notice the " Sei Sonate per Cembalo," dedicated to Frederick II. of Prussia (1742), and the Würtemberg Sonatas, published in 1745. Of his middle period, the " Sechs Sonaten fürs Clavier mit veränderten Reprisen," Berlin, 1760, and the " Sechs leichte Sonaten," Leipzig, 1766. And of his latter period, the six collections of " Sonaten für Kenner u. Liebhaber," published at Leipzig between 1779 and 1787. With regard, however, to the last-named, it must be remembered that some are of a comparatively early date. Thus the 3rd Sonata of the 3rd Collection, one of the finest of Bach's works, was composed in 1763, while the collection itself only appeared in 1781. But a table of dates will be given further on.

If some of the best sonatas written after 1760 be compared with those of 1742, there will be found in the later works more character in the subject-matter, also movements of greater length. Practice, too, had improved the composer's style of writing. The later Bach did not return to the principal theme in such a crude, nay, lawless, fashion as the following :—

(Frederick) Sonata I.   First Movement.

In these "Frederick" Sonatas there is as yet no tendency to enharmonic and other surprise modulation such as Bach afterwards displayed. Then as to technique, we find here octaves and large chords comparatively rare,[1] while scale passages are more restricted.   Like Beethoven, Emanuel Bach seized hold of additional notes to the keyboard.   In 1742 his highest and lowest notes, apparently, were—

but afterwards—

[1] Yet, curiously, there is no chord in the later sonatas so large as the two on page 29 (6th Sonata)—

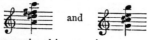

which, of course, are played in arpeggio,

In the introductory chapter we noted the change with regard to the number of movements of a sonata which took place between 1683, when Corelli published his first sonatas, and 1740, when E. Bach composed his first set. Instances were given of sonatas in three movements by Corelli, but with that composer *four* was the normal number; with E. Bach, *three*. This change came about in great measure through the concerto. From E. Bach, we are able to show the links in the chain of development: Bach, Haydn, Mozart, Beethoven; but though between Kuhnau, the first writer of sonatas for the clavier, and Bach, B. Pasquini wrote, as mentioned in the last chapter, sonatas in three movements, yet we have no knowledge that Bach was acquainted with them. Kuhnau, in fact, however interesting a phenomenon in the musical firmament, is not necessary to explain the appearance of Bach. Joh. Sebastian Bach was undoubtedly acquainted with the " Bible " Sonatas. He must have admired them, but he may have been afraid of the freedom of form which they displayed, and of their tendency to programme-music; and perhaps he did not speak of them to his sons, lest they should be led astray. For, as we have already mentioned, Sebastian Bach seems to have yielded for a moment to the Kuhnau influence, but, if we may judge from his subsequent art-work, he did not feel satisfied that it was a good one.

In 1742, E. Bach dedicated the six sonatas

(composed in 1740) to Frederick the Great.   The
title-page runs thus :—

Sei Sonate
per Cembalo
che all' Augusta Maestà
di
Frederico II.
Rè di Prussia
D. D. D.
l'Autore
Carlo Filippo Emanuele Bach
Musico di Camera di S.M.
Alle spese di Balth. Schmid
in Norimberga.

And in the obsequious dedication, the composer
describes them as works "debolissimo Talento
mio." As Bach's earliest published sonatas, they
are, for our purpose, of special interest. Their
order is as follows :—

Sonata	1, in F	Poco Allegro, Andante, Vivace.
„	2, „ B flat	Vivace, Adagio, Allegro assai.
„	3, „ E	Poco Allegro, Adagio, Presto.
„	4, „ C minor	Allegro, Adagio, Presto.
„	5, „ C	Poco Allegro, Andante, Allegro assai.
„	6, „ A	Allegro, Adagio, Allegro.

The first and last movements of all six are in
binary form. In the five major sonatas, the first
sections close in the key of the dominant, and in
the one minor sonata (No. 4), in the relative major.
The opening movement of each sonata is in early
sonata - form : the second section starts with the

principal theme, or a brief allusion to it; but then, after a short development with modulation, there is a return to the principal key and to the principal theme.[1] The final movements, on the other hand, are of the usual *suite* order. Of interest and, indeed, of importance in our history of development are the contents of the first section of the opening movements. In some of the Scarlatti sonatas (see No. 56) there is to be found a fairly definite second subject in the dominant key, or, in the case of a minor piece, in the dominant minor or relative major. Here the process of differentiation is continued; in the 2nd Sonata the contrast between the two subjects is specially marked. We give the opening bar of each—

In most of the developments the composer steers clear of the principal key, so that at the return of the principal theme it may appear fresh. To such a method, since Beethoven, we are quite accustomed; but it is curious how little

[1] Excepting in the fifth, which, by the way, was, for a long time, considered to be the compositon of J. S. Bach, and was published as such by J. C. Westphal & Co. This return to the opening theme is to be found already in the sonatinas for violin and cembalo by G. P. Telemann published at Amsterdam in 1718. See Allegro of No. 1, in A; the main theme is given as usual in the key of the dominant at the beginning of the second section. Then after a modulation to the key of the relative minor, a return is made to the opening key and the opening theme.

attention—even with the example of E. Bach before him—Haydn paid to such an effective means of contrast in some of his early sonatas. In Bach's No. 6, in A, the development assumes unusual magnitude; it is even longer than the first section.   And it is not only long, but interesting.   One passage, of which we quote a portion, has rather a modern appearance:[1]—

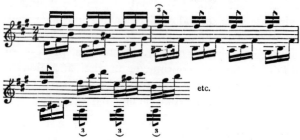

The return of the principal theme is preceded by an unexpected entry of the opening bars in B minor,—a first sign of that humour which afterwards formed so prominent a feature in Bach's music.   And the theme itself, after the opening notes, is dealt with in original fashion.

[1] Similar passages are to be found in the opening Vivace of J. G. Müthel's 2nd Sonata in G. He was a pupil of J. S. Bach, and either a pupil or close follower of E. Bach. His six published sonatas are of great musical interest ; in his wide sweeping arpeggios and other florid passages he shows an advance on E. Bach. His 2nd Arioso with twelve varations is worth the notice of pianists in search of something unfamiliar. There are features in the music—and of these the character of the theme is not least—which remind one strongly of Beethoven's 32 C minor variations.

The middle movements of Nos. 2, 3, 5, and 6 are in the key of the relative minor; that of No. 1 is in the tonic minor, and that of No. 4 (C minor), in the relative major. No. 1, twice interrupted by a recitative (upper part and figured bass),[1] is dignified, yet tender, and, in form, original. The Adagio, in C sharp minor, of No. 3 is a movement of singular charm; it is based on imitation, but, though old in style, it breathes something of the new spirit, or rather—for there is nothing new under the sun—of the old Florentine spirit which freed music for a time from the fetters of polyphony. The genius of Johann Sebastian Bach gained the victory over form, and, in fact, exhausted fugue-form. It is in the clever, but dry fugues of some of his contemporaries and, especially, successors, that one can feel the absolute necessity for a new departure. This Adagio is, as it were, a delicate remembrance, and one not unmixed with sadness, of the composer's immortal parent.

The light, lively final movements need no description. All the music of these sonatas is written in two or three parts or voices; occasionally there are chord passages in which for the moment the number is increased. We have dwelt somewhat in detail on this work, as it appears to be little known.

There is a sonata in the key of D major, published in the 3rd Collection (1763) of Marpurg's

---

[1] A recitative is also to be found in a Müller sonata.

Clavierstücke (p. 10), by E. Bach, which was
written in the same year (1740), but earlier than
the " Frederick " Sonatas.   C. H. Bitter remarks that
if the year of composition were not known, it would
certainly pass as a much later work.   The first
movement reminds one of Beethoven's terse, bold
style.   Bitter refers to the freedom with which the
thoughts are expressed, to the melodious character
of the Andante, and to the humour of the Finale.
He might also have referred to the style of writing
for the instrument, which suggests a later date.

In 1745 (?) appeared the Würtemberg Sonatas
(so called because they were dedicated to Bach's
pupil, the *Duca di Wirtemberg e Teckh*, as he is
named on the title-page of the original edition).
These sonatas are marked as Opera seconda.
They were offered by the composer to the Duke
in recognition of the many favours shown to him
" at the time when I had the honour of giving
you lessons in music at Berlin." [1]   Of these
sonatas we have only been able to have access to
the two preserved in the British Museum ; the
others are probably of similar character.

No. 1, in E flat, opens with an Adagio, followed
by an Allegro assai (E flat), and then by a
Menuet alternato and Trio, both in E flat, and
with the former *da capo*.   The first and second
movements are in old binary form ; the Allegro
shows the influence of D. Scarlatti.   The Minuet is

[1] " In tempo in cui ebbi l'onore di darle Lezzione di Musica in
Berlino,"

fresh and pleasing. It is evident, taking E. Bach himself as standard, that this is a suite rather than a sonata.

No. 2, in B flat, is of similar character and construction. Both sonatas are old in form, but more modern in their subject-material and style of writing than those dedicated to the King of Prussia. In the latter there is a solidity not to be found here; in its place we have lightness, almost merriment; they were written, one would almost think, expressly for the amusement of the Duke. The rapid semi-quaver passages (as in No. 1) and the crossing of hands (as in No. 2) tell in no undecided manner of the influence of Scarlatti. The exceedingly light and graceful Minuets remind one of the kinship between the composer and Haydn.

In a letter to Forkel, dated 10th February 1775, Bach writes as follows :—

" Die 2 Sonaten, welche Ihren Beyfall vor-züglich haben, sind die einzigen von dieser Art, die ich je gemacht habe. Sie gehören zu der, aus dem H-moll, die ich Ihnen mitschickte, zu der aus dem B, die Sie nun auch haben, u. zu 2en aus der Hafner-Würtembergischen Sammlung, u. sind alle 6 anno 1743, im Töplitzer Bade von mir, der ich damahls sehr gicht-brüchig war, auf einem Claviacord mit der kurzen Octav verfertiget." [1]

[1] " The two sonatas, which met with your special approval, are the only ones of this kind which I have ever composed. They are

It would be interesting to know the two sonatas belonging to this period, "the only ones of the kind that I have ever written." In the catalogue of musical remains of E. Bach, published two years after his death, the opening bars are given of a Sonata in B minor (see above letter) written at Töplitz in 1743—

This, surely, must be the one mentioned in the above letter.

In 1760, Bach published six sonatas with varied repeats (*mit veränderten Reprisen*), dedicated to Princess Amelia of Prussia. In the preface the composer remarks that " nowadays change or repetition is indispensable." He complains that some players will not play the notes as written, even the first time; and again, that players, if the changing on repetition is left to them, make alterations unsuitable to the character

connected with the one in B minor, which I sent to you, with the one in B flat, which you now have also, and with two out of the Hafner-Würtemberg Collection ; and all six were composed on a Claviacord with the short octave, at the Töplitz baths, when I was suffering from a severe attack of gout."

A series of six sonatas by E. Bach is in the *Trésor des Pianistes*, and is said to have been published at Nuremberg in 1744 ; the work is also dedicated to the Duke of Würtemberg, and the Opus number (2) is also given to it. There is mention of these sonatas in Bitter's biography of J. S. Bach's sons, but not of the others.

of the music. These sonatas are of great historic interest. This preface, also the evident necessity for additional (inner part) notes at times, especially in the slow movements of E. Bach and other composers of that day, make one feel that, as it now stands, much of Bach's music is a dead letter. Here we are face to face with a question which in a kindred matter has given rise to much controversy. If the music is to produce its proper effect, something must be done. To that (in the case of Emanuel Bach's sonatas) all reasonable musicians must agree. Yet not, perhaps, as to what that something should be. According to certain authorities, only additions should be made which are strictly in keeping with the spirit of the age in which the music was written. Some, on the other hand, would bring the music up to date ; they think it better to clothe eighteenth-century music in nineteenth-century dress, than to ask musicians with nineteenth-century ears to listen to patched-up eighteenth-century music. The second plan would not be approved by musicians who hold the classical masters in veneration ; with a little modification, the first one, however, ought to meet with general acceptance. We may write in keeping with the spirit of a past age, but the music must now be played on an instrument of different character, compass, and quality of tone ; so surely in making additions (and, so far as certain ornaments are concerned, alterations) these things ought to be taken into consideration. A certain latitude should, therefore,

be allowed to the transcriber ; hard-and-fast rules
in such a delicate task are impossible.   The late Dr.
Bülow edited six of Emanuel Bach's sonatas,[1] and
though he was well acquainted with the composer's
style of writing, his anxious desire to present the
music in the most favourable light sometimes led
him to make changes of which even lenient judges
would not approve.   The matter is an interesting
one, and we may therefore venture to refer somewhat in detail to one passage.   In the 3rd Sonata
(F minor) of the 3rd Collection, the passage—

has been changed by Bülow: he has altered the C flat
in the second half of the first bar into a C natural,
thus smoothing down the hard progression to the
key of B flat minor.   Now this very passage had
already, nearly a hundred years previously, attracted
the notice of Forkel, who admitted that, apart from
the context, it jarred against his musical feeling.
But he had thought over the composer's intention
in writing that sonata, and had come to the conclusion that, in the opening Allegro, Bach wished

[1] Sechs ausgewählte Sonaten für Klavier allem von Carl Philipp
Emanuel Bach bearbeitet und mit einem Vorwort herausgegeben
von Hans von Bülow (Peters, Leipzig).

to express indignation.[1]   He therefore asks : " Are
the hard, rough, passionate expressions of an
angry and indignant man beautiful ? "   In this case,
Forkel was of opinion that the hard modulation
was a faithful record of what the composer wished
to express.[2]   The natural order of history seems
inverted here.   One would have expected Forkel
to look upon the music from an abstract, but
Bülow from a poetical point of view.   C. H. Bitter
—also on purely musical grounds — condemns
Bülow's alterations.   He says:—"Even weaknesses
of great masters, among which the passages in
question are not to be counted, still more so,
special peculiarities, should be left untouched.
What would become of Beethoven, if each generation of musicians, according to individual judgment,
arrogated to itself the right, here and there, of ex-
punging hardnesses, smoothing down peculiarities,
and softening even sharp points with which, from
time to time, we come into unpleasant contact ?
Works of art must be accepted as they are."

The first part of Bitter's argument is sound ;
but, unfortunately for the last, the writer in his life
of Emanuel Bach and his brothers insists on the
necessity of *not* accepting Emanuel's clavier works
as they are.

He quotes a passage from the Andante of the
4th Sonata of the second set of the " Reprisen

1 In like manner he feels in the Andante, *reflection*, and in the
final Andantino, *melancholy consolation*.
  Leipziger Mus. Almanack, 1783.

Sonaten," and comes to the natural conclusion that
it was only an outline requiring filling up.

With all his faults, one cannot but admire the
spirit in which Bülow worked.   He felt the
greatness of the old masters, regretted the limited
means which they had at their command, also the
stenographic system in which they were accustomed
to express their thoughts ; and he sought, therefore,
to make use of modern   means, and thereby
was naturally tempted to introduce modern effects.
The restoration of the old masters is a difficult
and delicate task, and in most cases, one may add,
a thankless one.   In the matter of transcription,
however, it is important to distinguish between a
Bülow and a Tausig : the one displayed the intelli-
gence of an artist ;   the other, the thoughtlessness
of a *virtuoso*.

But what, it may be asked, is the character of
the changes made by Bach ?   The matter is of
interest ;   by examining these sonatas, we get
some idea of the difference between letter and
spirit.   However, from what we have said above, a
mere imitation of these changes, in playing Bach's
music, would, in its turn, be letter rather than spirit.

As a rule the bass remains the same, though
plain crotchets may become quavers, as in extract
from Sonata I given below, or notes turned into
broken octaves—

or, at times, some very slight alteration may
occur, such as—

In the upper parts the changes are similar to
those found in the variations of Haydn and
Mozart. An illustration will be better than any
explanation, and we accordingly give a brief
extract from the 1st Sonata: first the five bars
of the Allegretto, as at the opening, then as they
are changed—

The publication of the set of six Leipzig collections of sonatas, etc., commenced in 1779; but thirteen years previously, the composer had published a set of "Sechs Leichte Clavier Sonaten," and these, in one or two respects, are curious. The opening movement of No. 6 has no double bars, and, therefore, no repeat of the first section. And again, it has a coda pausing on the dominant chord and followed by an Andantino. This second movement, peculiar in form and modulation, ends on the dominant of F, leading directly to the Presto.

The opening of the Larghetto of No. 2—

etc.

was probably the prototype of many a theme of
the classical masters.

The works by which Emanuel Bach is best
known are the six collections of sonatas, rondos,
and fantasias published at Leipzig between 1779–
1787. The composer died in 1788. The 1st
Collection (1779) bears the title " Sechs Clavier-
sonaten für Kenner und Liebhaber," and, in fact,
contains six sonatas. But " nebst einigen Rondos "
(together with some Rondos) was already added
to the title-page of the 2nd and 3rd Collections ;
and to the remaining ones, the still further
addition of " Freye Fantasien."

For the sake of reference, the list of sonatas is
subjoined—

	Coll.				
(1779)	1	Sonata in C		1773	Hamburg.
	,,	,,	,, F	1758	Berlin.
	,,	,,	,, B minor	1774	Hamburg.
	,,	,,	,, A (Bülow No. 3)	1765	Potsdam.
	,,	,,	,, F	1772	Hamburg.
	,,	,,	,, G (Bülow No. 4)	1765	Potsdam.
(1780)	2	,,	,, G	1774	Hamburg.
	,,	,,	,, F	1780	Hamburg.
	,,	,,	,, A (Bülow No. 2)	1780	Hamburg.
(1781)	3	,,	,, A minor	1774	Hamburg.

Coll.

(1781)	3	Sonata in	D minor (Bülow No. 5)	1766	Potsdam.
	,,	,,	,, F minor (Bülow No. 1)	1763	Berlin.
(1783)	4	,,	,, G	1781	Hamburg.
	,,	,,	,, E minor	1765	Berlin.
(1785)	5	,,	,, E minor	1784	Hamburg.
	,,	,,	,, B flat	1784	Hamburg.
(1787)	6	,,	,, D	1785	Hamburg.
	,,	,,	,, E minor	1785	Hamburg.

Without copious musical examples, an analysis of these eighteen sonatas would prove heavy reading. It will, therefore, be easier for the writer, and certainly pleasanter for his readers, to give a somewhat " freye Fantasia " description of them, laying emphasis naturally on points connected with the special purpose in view.[1]

In the matter of tonality there are some curiosities. When Beethoven's 1st Symphony appeared, the opening bars of the introduction became stumbling-stones to the pedagogues of that day. The work was, without doubt, in the key of C major ; yet, instead of opening with the tonic chord of that key, the composer led up to it through the keys of the subdominant, relative

[1] The number of sonatas in each collection grew gradually smaller : first six, then three, lastly two. The dates of composition in the last column of above table may be studied with advantage : a later date of publication does not necessarily imply a more advanced work. Thus, of the three fine sonatas in the 3rd Collection (all of which are included in the Bülow selection), one was written eighteen, another fifteen, and the third (though first in order of reckoning), seven years before the date of publication (1781).

minor, and dominant. No wonder that such a proceeding surprised conventional minds, and that the critics warned Beethoven of the danger of "going his own way." But his predecessor, Emanuel Bach, had also strayed from the peda-gogic path, a narrow one, yet, in the end, leading to destruction. In the first book (1779), the 5th Sonata (as shown by the whole of the move-ment, with exception of the two opening bars) is in the key of F major, yet the first bar is in C minor (minor key of the dominant) and the second, in D minor (relative minor of the principal key).

There were, no doubt, respecters of tonality also in Emanuel Bach's day, to whom such free measures must have seemed foolhardy. While composing this sonata Bach was, apparently, in daring mood. The slow middle movement in

D minor opens with an inversion of the dominant ninth, and the Finale in F thus—

Of the character of the first section of movements in binary form we have already spoken in the introductory chapter.

In the matter of development, the Bach sonatas are in one respect particularly striking; the composer seems to have resolutely turned away from the fugal style, and in so doing probably found himself somewhat hampered. Like the early Florentine reformers, Bach was breaking with the past, and with a mightier past than the one on which the Florentines turned their back; like them, he, too, was occupied with a new form. Not the music itself of the first operas, but the spirit which prompted them, is what we now admire; in E. Bach, too,— especially when viewed in the light of subsequent history,—we at times take the will for the deed.

We meet with much the same kinds of development as in Scarlatti: phrases or passages taken bodily from the first section and repeated on different degrees of the scale, extensions of phrases, and passage-writing based on some figure from the exposition, etc. The short development section of the Sonata in G (Collection No. 6) offers examples of the three methods of development

just mentioned. Bach, like Scarlatti, was a master
of his instrument, and even when—as was said of
Mendelssohn—he had nothing particular to say,
he always managed to say that little well. E. Bach
has already much to suffer in the inevitable comparison with Beethoven ; and the fact that we have
the full message of the one, but not of the other,
no doubt accentuates the difference.

In many ways Bach reminds one of Beethoven.
There are unexpected fortes and pianos, unexpected crescendos and diminuendos. Of such, the
noble Larghetto in F minor of the Sonata in F
(Collection 1779, No. 2) offers, indeed, several fine
examples. Particularly would we notice the passage
just before the return of the opening theme ; it
begins *ff*, but there is a gradual decrease to *pp* ; the
latter seems somewhat before its time, and therefore surprises. Then, again, we meet with out-of-the-
way modulations. Bach was extremely fond of
enharmonic transitions,[1] and the same can be said
of Beethoven in both his early and his late works.
The means employed by the two composers may
be the same, but the effect is, of course, always
more striking in Beethoven, whose thoughts were
deeper, and whose means of expressing them were
in every way more extended. And once again, in
some of the forms of melody, in figures and passages,
traces can be found of connection between the two
masters. To our thinking the bond of union
between E. Bach and Beethoven is stronger than

[1] See particularly the Sonata in G (collection of 1783).

the oft-mentioned one between the early master and Haydn : Haydn was practically Bach's pupil ; Beethoven, his spiritual heir.   This it is which gives interest to any outward resemblances which may be detected, not the resemblances themselves.

In Bach's six sonatas of 1742 the movements are detached.   But the opening movement (an Andante in sonata form) of the 2nd Sonata of the Leipzig Collection of 1779 ends with a few bars in canonic form (and with quaint Bebung effect), leading without break to the following Larghetto.   The next sonata also connects the second with the third movement.   In the above case the change was merely from the key of tonic major to that of minor ; but here the movement is in G minor, and an enharmonic modulation leads to the dominant of B minor, key of the final movement.   The sonata begins in B minor, and the choice of the remote key of G minor for the middle movement is somewhat curious.   Sonata No. 4 connects first and second movements; and the third is evidently meant to follow without pause. It must, however be remembered that the majority of the Leipzig sonatas do not have the various movements thus connected.   It therefore seems to have been an experiment rather than a settled plan.   Examples of the connection of movements are also to be found in Nichelmann and J. C. F. Bach.   The same thing may be seen in some of Haydn's sonatas (Nos. 18, 22, etc.), while Beethoven offers a remarkable instance in his sonata, Op. 57.

The 1st Sonata of the 2nd Collection passes from the first to the second movement (Allegretto, G minor; Larghetto, F sharp minor) in a curious manner, by enharmonic means. The last bar has—

The quotation is in abbreviated form. The second chord would, of course, be taken at first as dominant minor ninth on G. The 1st Sonata of the 4th Collection is not striking as music, and certainly not of sufficient importance to justify serious inquiry into the peculiar order of keys for the three movements (G, G minor, and E major).

With regard to the number of movements, all except two of the eighteen sonatas have three; the second and third of the 2nd Collection have only two.

John Christian Bach, or the " London " Bach, as he was called, dedicated his fifth work, consisting of six sonatas " Pour le clavecin ou pianoforte," to Ernst, Duke of Mecklenburg. This cannot have been before 1759, as that was the year in which the composer came to London. He describes himself on the title-page as—" Maître de Musique de S. M. la Reine d'Angleterre." These sonatas, as

we learn from the dedication, were written for
the " amusement " of the Duke.   The first,
third, and fourth have each only two movements.   They remind us less of E. Bach than of
Haydn's early style.   There is some very fresh,
pleasing writing in them.   No. 5 has some excellent
practising passages, and perhaps the following—

 etc.

may have suggested to Cramer his first study.
The middle movement of No. 6 is a vigorous
double Fugue; the whole sonata is, indeed, one of
the finest of the set.

A Sonata in D, by Wilhelm Friedmann Bach, is
commented on by Dr. Parry in his " Sonata "
dictionary article.   There is another one in C
major, a fresh and vigorous example of a musician
whose powers were never fully developed.

The sonatas of Pietro Domenico Paradies (*b.*
1710), a contemporary of E. Bach, are of interest.
They were published in London by John Johnson,
and bear the title, " Sonate di gravicembalo dedicate
a sua altezza reale la principessa da Pier Domenico
Paradies Napolitano."   The edition bears no date ;
but the right of printing and selling granted by
George II. bears the date November 28, 1754.
A second edition was published at Amsterdam in
1770.   The sonatas are twelve in number, and
consist of only two movements of various character :

some have an Allegro or Presto, followed by a Presto, Allegro, or Gigue ; and sometimes (as in Nos. 9 and 11) the second movement is an Andante. In other sonatas the first movement is in slow time. These two-movement sonatas would seem to form an intermediate stage between Scarlatti and Emanuel Bach. As a matter of fact, however, the latter, as we have seen, had published clavier sonatas in three movements long before the appearance of those of Paradies. In some of the movements in binary form Paradies shows an advance on Scarlatti (see Nos. 1 and 10), for in the second section there is a return, after modulation, to the principal theme. Some have the theme in the dominant key at the commencement of that section, others not. Thus we see various stages represented in these sonatas. The music is delightfully fresh, and, from a technical point of view, interesting. The influence of Scarlatti both in letter and spirit is strongly felt. In some of the movements (*cf.* first movement of No. 8 and of No. 12) there is a feature which Paradies did not inherit from Scarlatti, *i.e.* the so-called Alberti bass. Of such a bass Scarlatti gives only slight hints. Alberti, said to have been its inventor, was a contemporary of Paradies, and the latter may have learnt the trick from him : there are many examples of its use. In Alberti, " VIII Sonate Opera Prima," [1] the opening Allegro of No. 2 has

---

[1] All of these consist of two movements ; in the first, both movements are marked Andante.

it in forty-four of the forty-six bars of which it
consists, and, besides, each section is repeated.
That convenient form of accompaniment soon
came into vogue.   It occurs frequently in the
sonatas and concertos of J. C. Bach and Haydn,
but it is in the works of second-rate composers that
one sees the full use, or rather abuse, made of it.
No. 8 of the Paradies sonatas is particularly
attractive, and the second movement forms a not
unpleasant reminiscence of Handel's so-called
" Harmonious Blacksmith " variations.

CHAPTER V

HAYDN AND MOZART

I.—Haydn

THIS composer, to whom is given the name of "father of the symphony and the quartet," was born at Rohrau, a small Austrian village on the Leitha, in the night between 31st March and 1st April 1732. At a very early age the boy's sweet voice attracted the notice of G. Reuter, capellmeister of St. Stephen's, Vienna, and for many years he sang in the cathedral choir. In 1749 he was dismissed, the alleged cause being a practical joke played by him on one of his fellow-choristers. He was, as Sir G. Grove relates in his article "Haydn" in the *Dictionary of Music and Musicians*, thrown upon the world "with an empty purse, a keen appetite, and no friends." Haydn took up his abode in an attic in the old Michaelerhaus. But it chanced that Metastasio lived in the same building, and the famous poet took an interest in the penniless composer, and, among other things, taught him Italian. Metastasio was extremely fond of music, and we know from his letters that the flowing compositions of his countrymen delighted him more than the learned music of Germany. Then Haydn made the acquaintance of Porpora, who gave him instruction in composition and in the art of singing. And he is also supposed to have studied the works of San Martini, an Italian composer in the service of Prince Esterhazy. In addition, Italian music was much played and much admired in Vienna. Emanuel Bach also, as we have seen, came under Italian influence, but not until he had finished his studies under his father's guidance. Once more, we may conclude that Haydn, before he commenced writing clavier sonatas, had made acquaintance with those of Paradies and of Alberti. These early Italian influences should be noted, for one is apt to think rather of the young composer as plodding through Fux's " Gradus " and playing Emanuel Bach's sonatas on his " little worm-eaten clavier." During his last years Haydn told his friend Griesinger that he had diligently studied Emanuel Bach, and that he owed very much to him. From the painter Dies, in his biographical notice of the master, we also learn how fond he was of playing Emanuel Bach's sonatas. And this influence was undoubtedly not only a strong, but a lasting one ; in 1788, the year in which E. Bach died, Haydn wrote to Artaria, begging the latter to send him that master's last two works for clavier.

In reference to Haydn, musicians are apt to speak merely of his sonatas, whereas those of Beethoven are generally described by their key, or

their opus number ; or as belonging to one of the
three periods into which that master's art-work is
usually divided.   There is good reason for this
difference.   Haydn's sonatas are not of equal
importance with those of his successor ; and then
some are old-fashioned, others second-rate.   Beethoven's sonatas are by no means all of equal
merit, yet there is not one but has some feature,
whether of form, or development, or technique, by
which it may be distinguished.   And yet a close and
careful study of Haydn's sonatas will show that he,
too, had his periods of apprenticeship, mastery, and
maturity.   Let not our readers take alarm.   We
are not going to analyse his thirty-five sonatas, or
to enter into minute details.   But we shall try, by
selecting some of the most characteristic works, to
show how the master commenced, continued, and
concluded.

The earliest of the published sonatas,[1] No. 1
(33), is somewhat of a curiosity.   It consists of
four movements : an Allegro in G major ; a
Minuetto and Trio, G major and minor ; an
Adagio in G minor ; and an Allegro molto in G
major.   It is the only sonata of Haydn's which
contains four movements.   The plaintive Trio
and the Scarlatti-like Finale are attractive.

In the year 1774, J. J. Hummel, at Amsterdam,
published six sonatas, the last three of which

[1] For the benefit of readers who may not possess Pohl's *J.
Haydn,* we insert in brackets, after the Pohl numbers, those of the
Holle edition.

appear to have been originally written for pianoforte and violin;[1] and in 1776 six more were
printed by Longman & Broderip as Op. 14.
These may serve as specimens of Haydn's early
style; and in them, by the way, the composer was
accused of imitating, nay, caricaturing, E. Bach.

In the *European Magazine* for October 1784
there appeared an account of Joseph Haydn, "a
celebrated composer of music," in which occurs
the following :—

" Amongst the number of professors who wrote
against our rising author was Philipp Emanuel
Bach of Hamburgh (formerly of Berlin); and the
only notice Haydn took of their scurrility and
abuse was to publish lessons written in imitation
of the several styles of his enemies, in which their
peculiarities were so closely copied, and their ex-
traneous passages (particularly those of Bach of
Hamburgh) so inimitably burlesqued, that they all
felt the poignancy of his musical wit, confessed its
truth, and were silent."

Further on the writer mentions the sonatas of
Ops. 13 and 14 as " expressly composed in order
to ridicule Bach of Hamburgh"; nay, he points to
the second part of the second sonata in Op. 13 and
the whole of the third sonata in the same work
by way of special illustration.

---

[1] Cf. C. F. Pohl's *J. Haydn*, vol. ii. p. 311.   They are in the
keys of D, E flat, and A, and are interesting.   The Tempo di
Menuetto of the second presents a strict canon in the octave.   In
the last, too, there is a curious canon.

There are many resemblances to E. Bach in Haydn,—notes wide apart, pause bars, surprise modulations, etc.,—and this is not more extraordinary than to find resemblances between Mozart and Beethoven ; but the charge of caricature seems unfair. Besides, it is scarcely likely that Haydn, who owed so much to Bach, would have done any such thing. It must be remembered that at the date of the *European Magazine* in question, E. Bach had not yet published any of the six Leipzig Collections (" Sonaten für Kenner," etc.), by which he is best known at the present day.

Of the six sonatas, Op. 13, the first three are Nos. 8 (26), 9 (27), 10 (28) in Pohl's thematic catalogue (*Joseph Haydn*, vol. ii.). The other three have not been reprinted in modern collections. In the first three the keys and order of movements are as follow :—

No. 1. Allegro moderato in C ; Adagio, F ; Finale, Presto.
No. 2. Allegro moderato in E ; Andante, E minor ; Finale, Tempo di Menuetto.
No. 3. Allegro moderato in F ; Larghetto, E minor ; Presto.

These sonatas are interesting as music, and the workmanship is skilful. If one can get over the thinness of the part-writing, especially in the slow movements, there is much to enjoy in them. The style of movement—Tempo di Menuetto—in No. 2 recalls Emanuel Bach's "Würtemberg" sonatas of 1745.

Here are the numbers of the sonatas of Op.

14: 11 (20), 12 (21), 13 (22), 14 (23), 15 (24),
16 (25).   And here are the keys and movements—

No. 1. Allegro con brio in G ; Minuetto, G ; Trio, G minor ;
    Presto.
No. 2. Allegro moderato in E flat ; Minuetto, E flat ; Trio,
    E flat minor ; Presto.
No. 3. Moderato in F ; Adagio, B flat ; Tempo di Menuetto.
No. 4. Allegro in A ; Adagio ; Tempo di Minuetto con
    Variazione.
No. 5. Moderato in E ; Presto.
No. 6. Allegro moderato in B minor ; Tempo di Minuetto ;
    Presto.

During the eighteenth century, both in Italy
and Germany, sonatas in two movements were
common, but with Haydn the reduction in No. 5
probably was made on practical, and not artistic
grounds. Schindler once asked Beethoven why
he had only two movements to his Sonata in C
minor (Op. 111), and the master replied—probably
with a twinkle in his eye—that he had not had
time for a third.

If these sonatas of 1776 be compared with
earlier ones (1767), an immense improvement in
the development sections will be observed. In
the earliest but one of the master's sonatas—No.
2 (30)—the whole of the middle section is in the
principal key. No. 4 (Op. 14) has all three
movements connected,—a plan, as we have already
seen, adopted by E. Bach in some of his sonatas.
The sonata in question is in the key of A major.
The Allegro ends with an arpeggio dominant

chord, and still in the same bar follows the
dominant chord of the relative key of F sharp
minor, leading directly to the Adagio; this movement, in its turn, closes on the dominant chord
of A, the key, of course, of the final movement
(Tempo di Minuetto con Variazioni).

In 1780 six sonatas were published by Artaria,
and dedicated to the sisters Franziska and Mari-
anne v. Auenbrugger. They are Nos. 20 (1),
21–24 (10–13), and 7 (14). No. 20 (1) is a
bright little work. No. 21 (10) (C sharp minor)
opens with an interesting movement.[1]   The
sonata ends with a beautiful Menuetto and Trio, in
which the composer comes very near to Beethoven.
The middle movement is a Scherzando, and thereby hangs a little tale. No. 24 (13) commences
with the same theme. When Haydn sent the
sonatas to his publisher he called attention to
this resemblance, and, in fact, requested that it
should be mentioned on the inner side of the
title-page. And he added: " I could, of course,
have chosen a hundred other ideas in place of
this one; but in order not to run any risk of
blame on account of this intentional trifle (which
the critics, and especially my enemies, will regard
in a bad light), I make this *avertissement*. Or
please add some note of a similar kind, otherwise
it may prove detrimental to the sale." No. 22
(11) has an opening Allegro in Haydn's brightest

[1] The treble of the tenth bar of the second section has been
frequently printed a third too high.

manner.   The short Largo is quaint and expressive; the *ff* chord of the Neapolitan sixth is
of fine effect.   The movement ends on the dominant chord, and thus leads without break to the
lively Presto Finale.   The concluding movement
of the next sonata displays a crispness and vigour
which remind one of Haydn's great successor.
Already in connection with these six sonatas
have we mentioned Beethoven.   And from this
period onwards the kinship between the two
composers becomes more evident.   Haydn, however, did not, like Beethoven, rise steadily higher
and higher; great moments came, as it were, by
fits and starts.   He wrote in season and out of
season ; *nulla dies sine linea* seems to have been
his motto.   With Beethoven, a later work, unless
it be one of his few *pièces d'occasion*, means a fuller
revelation of his genius.

We will now pass on to the latest period,
represented by two great sonatas, both in the key
of E flat.   The one was written for the composer's
friend and patron, Frau v. Genziger.   The opening Allegro shows earnest, deep feeling, while at
the close of the recapitulation Haydn makes us
feel the full power of his genius; the passage
irresistibly recalls moments in the first movement
of the " Appassionata "; those stately reiterated
chords, those solemn pauses, have a touch of
mystery about them.   It is interesting to see how
the second theme is evolved from the principal
subject of the movement; by a slight modification

the character of the music is quite changed; what was stately is now light and graceful. The Adagio cantabile is one of the purest examples of a style of music which has become a thing of the past. The full and sustained tone of modern instruments has rendered unnecessary those turns, arpeggios, and numerous ornaments with which the composers of the last century tried to make amends for the fleeting tones of their harpsichords and clavichords. Haydn and Mozart were skilful in this art of embellishment, though sometimes it was unduly profuse; this Adagio of Haydn's is a model of sobriety. The bold minor section, which Frau v. Genziger, by the way, found rather troublesome to play, offers an effective contrast to the major. A graceful Tempo di Menuetto brings the work to an effective close. The other Sonata in E flat[1] is much more difficult to play. The writing is fuller, and it contains passages which even a modern pianist need not disdain. It is really strange that the sonata is not sometimes heard at the Popular Concerts. In the opening Allegro the exposition section contains more than the two orthodox themes, and the development

[1] This Sonata in E flat (Op. 78) was dedicated to Mrs. Bartolozzi, wife of the famous engraver, and to her Haydn also dedicated one in C major, marked as Op. 79,—a bright, clever and showy work, in which the influence of Clementi is sensibly felt. The development section of the opening Allegro, together with the return to the principal theme, is interesting. The Adagio, in the key of the subdominant, is one of Haydn's best, while the final movement (Allegro molto) is full of life and humour.

section assumes considerable magnitude; the latter is full of clever details and bold modulations. The key of the Adagio is E major, but this is of course the enharmonic equivalent of F flat. Brahms, in his last Sonata for Violoncello and Pianoforte in F, has the slow movement in F sharp. This has been spoken of as a novelty, yet Haydn, as we see, had already made the experiment; and similar instances may be found in Schubert and Beethoven, though not in their pianoforte sonatas. The Finale Presto reminds one by the style of writing, and by a certain quaint humour, of Emanuel Bach; but there are some bold touches—*sforzandos* on unaccented beats, prolongation of phrases, long dwelling on one harmony, etc.—which anticipate Beethoven. Traces of the past, foreshadowings of the future; these are familiar facts in evolution.

II.—Mozart

Before Mozart had reached the age of twenty he wrote six sonatas for a certain ·Baron Dürnitz, who, by the way, forgot to send the promised payment in return. Of these, Otto Jahn remarks that " their healthy freshness and finished form entitle them still to be considered as the best foundation for a musical education." Freshness is indeed the best term to describe both the thematic material and the developments. Four of them (Nos. 1, 2, 3, and 5) consist of the usual three movements; No. 4 commences with a long

Adagio in two sections, each of which is repeated.
Two graceful Minuets (the second taking the
place of a Trio) follow, and the third movement is
an Allegro in sonata-form. No. 6 has for its second
movement a Rondeau en Polonaise, and for its
third, a Theme with variations. The Rondo of
No. 3 (in B flat) is unusually long; it contains
two episodes, one in the relative minor, the other
in the subdominant. The next three sonatas (in
C, A minor, and D) are of greater importance.
They are all said to have been written at Mannheim. The first was most probably the one
mentioned in a letter of 1777 written by Mozart
to his father. He describes a public concert
given on the 22nd of October, and says : " Then
I played alone the last Sonata in D, then my Concerto in B flat, then a Fugue in C minor, and a
splendid Sonata in C major out of my own head,
with a Rondo at the end." The " last Sonata in
D " was the last of the set of six noticed above.
In reference to the Sonata in C, the expression
" out of my own head " would seem to indicate
that it had not at that time been written out.
Mozart was right to speak of the work as
" splendid." The bold opening subject, the well-
contrasted second theme, the short but masterly
development, the original leading back to the
principal subject, and the many variations in the
recapitulation section, fully justify his qualification.
The slow movement is full of charm, and the
Rondo, with its elaborate middle section, is of the

highest interest.   The 2nd Sonata, in A minor,
is, next to the one in C minor, Mozart's finest
effort in this department of musical literature.
And there is a story connected with it.   Capellmeister Cannabich's eldest daughter Rosa had
captivated the young composer ; he wrote to his
father about her, and described her as " a pretty,
charming girl," and added, " she has a staid
manner and a great deal of sense for her age (the
young lady was only thirteen); she speaks but
little, and when she does speak, it is with grace
and amiability."   On the very next day after his
arrival in Mannheim he began to write this
sonata for her.   The Allegro was finished in one
day.   Young Danner, the violinist, asked him
about the Andante, and Mozart replied: " I mean
to make it exactly like Mdlle. Rose herself."
This was the picture to which he worked.   One
of Beethoven's finest sonatas, the C sharp minor,
was inspired by a beautiful girl : a strong appeal
to the emotions calls forth a composer's best
powers.   Mozart's first movement was written on
31st October, and the Rondo on 8th November.   The
Allegro maestoso presents many points of interest.
The opening theme with its dotted motive is
prominent throughout the movement ; the transition passage to the key of the relative major is
based on it, and so is the coda to the exposition
section.   Again, in the development and recapitulation sections it forms a striking feature, while
in the final coda it is intensified by reiteration of

the dotted figure, and also by the rise from the
dominant to the tonic.   The slow movement, with
its expressive themes, graceful ornamentation, and
bold middle section, was not surpassed by Mozart
even in his C minor Sonata.   The Presto closes
the work in worthy manner ; it forms a contrast
to the first movement, and yet is allied to it in
sentiment.   The passionate outburst at the close,
with the repeated E's, seems almost a reminiscence
of the Allegro theme.   There are two features in
the development section of that movement which
point to Beethoven : the one is the augmentation
in the seventh bar of the quaver figure in the two
preceding bars ; the other, the phrase containing
the shake which is evolved from an earlier one by
curtailment of its first note.   The 3rd Sonata,
though in many ways attractive, will not bear comparison with the other two.   In 1779, at Vienna,
Mozart composed, among other sonatas, the beautiful one in A major,—the first example, perhaps, of
a sonata commencing with a theme and variations.
This first movement is very charming, but the
gem of the work is the delicate Menuetto; the
Trio speaks in tender, regretful tones of some
happy past.   The Alla Turca is lively, but not
far removed from the commonplace.

From among the symphonies of Mozart, the
three (in G minor, E flat, and C) which he wrote
in 1788 stand out with special prominence; and
so, from the sonatas, do the three in A minor
(1778), C minor (1784), and F (1788).   In the

first, as regards the writing, virtuosity asserts itself, and in the third, contrapuntal skill; but in the second, the greatness of music makes us forget the means by which that greatness is achieved. The Sonatas in A minor and F are wonderful productions, yet they stand a little lower than the C minor. The nobility and earnestness of the last-named give it a place near to Beethoven's best sonatas. We might say equal, were it not that the writing for the instrument is comparatively thin; however noble the ideas, they are but inadequately expressed. This C minor Sonata is remarkable for its originality, simplicity, and unity; Mozart possessed qualities which mark creative art of the highest kind. In writing some of his pianoforte sonatas, he had the public, or pupils, more or less in his mind; and though he did not become a mere sonata-maker, like some of his contemporaries, his whole soul was not always in his work; of this the inequalities in his music give evidence. In some movements (especially the closing ones) of the sonatas, the subject-matter is often trivial, and the passage-writing commonplace. The silkworm produces its smooth, regular ball of silk without effort, and in like manner Mozart could turn out Allegros, Rondos, sets of variations *à discretion*. The Sonata in C minor, to our thinking, is the only one in which he was entirely absorbed in his art; the only one in which the ideal is never marred by the real. The last movement is no mere Rondo, but one which stands in close relationship to the opening Allegro; they both have the same tragic spirit; both seem the outpouring of a soul battling with fate. The slow movement reveals Mozart's gift of melody and graceful ornamentation, yet beneath the latter runs a vein of earnestness; the theme of the middle section expresses subdued sadness. The affinity between this work and Beethoven's sonata (Op. 10, No. 1) in the same key is very striking.

Mozart composed his C minor Sonata towards the end of the year 1784. The C minor Fantasia, which precedes it in some editions, was not written until the middle of 1785. The two, however, were published together by Mozart himself. It is impossible to consider this a new experiment in sonata-form, as regards grouping of movements; the unity of character and feeling between Fantasia and Sonata no doubt led to their juxtaposition. The Fantasia is practically complete in itself; so too is the Sonata. The two are printed separately in Breitkopf & Härtel's edition of Mozart's works.

Haydn and Mozart represent an important stage in sonata history: they stand midway between Emanuel Bach and Beethoven. It is usual to look upon Bach as the founder, Haydn and Mozart as the builders-up, and Beethoven as the perfecter of the sonata edifice. Such a summing-up is useful in that it points to important landmarks in the evolution of the sonata; yet it is only a rough - and - ready one. Bach was something more than a founder, while

Beethoven, to say the least, shook the foundations of the edifice. Haydn and Mozart would seem to be fairly described, for traces of scaffolding are all too evident in their works, yet they found the building already raised. Some of it, however, appeared to them in rococo style, and so they gradually rebuilt. And they not only altered, but enlarged and strengthened. Of rebuilding and alteration, their slow movements and finales give evidence; and of enlargement, all the three sections of movements in so-called sonata-form. Their subject-matter, as it grew in importance, grew in compass. This in itself, of course, enlarged the exposition section; but the transition passage from first to second theme, and the rounding-off of the section, both grew in proportion. The joints, too, of the structure were strengthened: the half cadence no longer sufficed to divide first from second subject, or, after development, to return to the principal theme; then, again, the wider scope of the development itself demanded more striking harmonies, more forcible figuration, and more varied cadences.

The subject-matter, we have said, became more important; it differed also in character. The themes of Emanuel Bach, for the most part, seem to be evolved from harmonic progressions and groupings of notes; those of his successors, rather the source whence springs melody and figuration. The one uttered broken phrases; the others, complete musical sentences. Italian fashion prevailed during the second half of the eighteenth century much as it did in the first. The simple charm and warmth of the music of the violin-composers had penetrated the contrapuntal crust which covered Emanuel Bach's heart; and the feeling that he could never hope to rival his father must have rendered him all the more willing to yield to it. But the influence of his father could not be wholly cast aside, and Emanuel was, as it were, drawn in opposite directions; it is really wonderful what he actually achieved. True lovers of John Sebastian Bach know well that his music, though of a contrapuntal character, is by no means dry; but the formal aspect of it must have made its mark on the son ere he could feel the power, and realise the splendour of his father's genius.

Haydn and Mozart, on the other hand, were born and bred in the very midst of Italian music. Of Haydn's early days we have already spoken, and those of Mozart were not unsimilar. Otto Jahn, in his life of that composer, says of the father Leopold, that " his ideas were firmly rooted in the traditions of Italian music "; so firmly, indeed, that he could not appreciate the mild innovations of a Gluck. This paternal influence was deepened, besides, by Mozart's early visits to Italy.

Then, again, so far as we can make out, the clavier compositions of John Sebastian Bach, and, especially the "Well-tempered Clavier," were unknown both to Haydn and Mozart in their days of childhood and early manhood. What a difference in the case of Beethoven, who, it will be remembered, could play the greater number of the forty-eight Preludes and Fugues before he was twelve years of age! The beauty of Italian music not only impressed Haydn and Mozart, but kindled their creative faculties; while its simple, rhythmical character probably aided them materially in giving utterance to their thoughts and feelings. Nature had bestowed on them in rich measure the gift of melody, and they soon began to compose.

Emanuel Bach, we have said, was drawn in two opposite directions. Haydn and Mozart, though they were spared this dual influence, had, however, to face a difficulty. They found a form ready to hand, yet one which, as we have attempted to show, required modifications of various kinds. The former had to make the old fit in with the new; but the latter, the new with the old. Hence their inspiration was handicapped. They were to some extent constructing as well as creating; and then their sense of order, balance, and proportion was so strong, that they often turned out movements more remarkable for their clearness of form than for the strength of their contents.

Mozart profited by Haydn's early attempts, and his best sonatas are vastly superior to most of Haydn's. After Mozart's death, and even for some years before, Haydn seemed to have caught much of the spirit of the younger composer. He showed this especially in his London symphonies, but also in one or two of his later sonatas. " This mutual reaction," says Jahn, " so generously acknowledged by both musicians, must be taken into account in forming a judgment on them."

Haydn, though fully conscious of his own powers, practically acknowledged the superiority of his brother-artist. On learning of Mozart's death, he exclaimed : " Posterity will not see such talent for a century to come ! "——a prophecy which, at the time it was uttered, seemed likely of fulfilment.

CHAPTER VI

PREDECESSORS OF BEETHOVEN

I. Muzio Clementi

MUZIO CLEMENTI, born at Rome in 1752, was brought to England by Alderman Beckford, father of the author of *Vathek*, and at Fonthill Abbey he had leisure to study the works of Handel, John Sebastian Bach, Emanuel Bach, Domenico Scarlatti, and Paradies. Clementi, like Scarlatti, was a *virtuoso*; but although both indulged largely in technical display, they were true and intelligent artists. In Scarlatti, the balance between his musical ideas and the form in which they were presented was almost perfect; in Clementi, virtuosity often gained the ascendency over virtue. With the latter, however, as indeed with E. Bach, Haydn, Mozart, and many other composers, the necessity of earning a living, and therefore of writing for "long" ears, mixed with the love of fame, produced works which, like the old Eden tree, contained both good and evil. To judge such great men really fairly, the chaff ought to be separated from the wheat; and the

chaff ought to be thoroughly removed, even at the
risk of sometimes losing a portion of wheat.

To the true lover of music, choice selections are
more precious than complete collections ; the latter
are, of course, necessary to those whose business it
is to study the rise and development of the various
composers. The pianoforte sonatas of Mozart,
Haydn, Dussek, and Clementi might be reduced
to very moderate compass. To suggest that any
one of Beethoven's thirty-two should be removed
out of its place would now sound flat blasphemy ;
but art progresses, and some even now are falling
into oblivion. The catalogue of music performed
at the Popular Concerts during the history of the
past thirty-five years shows pretty clearly which
sonatas of Beethoven are likely to live long, and
which not. But to return to Clementi. He
published his first three sonatas (Op. 2, Nos. 1–3)
in 1770, the year in which Beethoven was born ;
and the influence which he exerted over that
master was considerable. In Beethoven's library
were to be found many sonatas of Clementi, and
the master's predilection for them is well known.
The world seldom renders full justice to men who
prepared the way for greater than themselves ;
Pachelbel, Böhm, and Buxtehude, the immediate
predecessors of Bach, and, again, Emanuel Bach,
to whom Haydn was so indebted, and whose
works were undoubtedly studied by Beethoven,
are notable examples. This is, of course, perfectly
natural : the best only survives ; but musicians who

take serious interest in their art ought, from time
to time, to look back and see how much was
accomplished and suggested by men who, in comparison with their mighty contemporaries and
successors, are legitimately ranked as second-rate.
Among such, Clementi holds high place. Beethoven over-shadowed the Italian composer; but the
harsh judgment expressed by Mozart[1] has contributed not a little, we imagine, to the indifference
now shown to the Clementi sonatas.[2] The judgment was a severe one; but Otto Jahn relates how
Clementi told his pupil Berger that, "at the period
of which Mozart writes, he devoted his attention to
brilliant execution, and in particular to double runs
and extemporised passages."   And, again, Berger
himself was of opinion that the sonata selected for
performance by Clementi at the memorable contest with Mozart in presence of the Emperor
Joseph the Second (December 1781), was decidedly inferior to his earlier compositions of the
same kind.   The sonata in question was the one
in B flat (B. & H., No. 61 ; Holle, No. 37), of
which the opening theme commences in the same
manner as the Allegro of the Overture to the
Magic Flute.   Mozart suffered much from the
predominant Italian influence at court, and the

[1] "Clementi is a charlatan, *like all the Italians*" (Letter to his
sister, June 7, 1783).

[2] It is thirty-five years since the fine one in B minor was performed at the Popular Concerts; and eighteen, since a Clementi
sonata has appeared on a Popular Concert programme.

" like all the Italians " in the letter just mentioned shows, to say the least, a bitter spirit. But the letter was a private one, probably hastily written. The judgment expressed was formed from an inferior work; in any case, it must not be taken too seriously. Mozart, by the way, was not the only composer who failed to render justice to his contemporaries.

Clementi's sonatas may be roughly divided into three classes. Some he wrote merely for the display of technique, while some were composed for educational purposes. But there remain others in which his heart and soul were engaged, and in these he reaches a very high level. Our classification is a rough one, for often in those which we consider his best, there is plenty of showy technique. With the exception of Mozart's sonata in C minor, and Haydn's " Genziger " and " London " sonatas, both in E flat, also some of Rust's, of which we shall soon have something to say, there are, to our thinking, none which in spirit come nearer to Beethoven than some of Clementi's. Mr. E. Dannreuther, in his article on the composer in Sir George Grove's *Dictionary of Music and Musicians*, justly remarks " that a judicious selection from his entire works would prove a boon."

In order to trace the relationship between Clementi and Beethoven, it may be well to state that Clementi in 1783 had published up to Op. 11 (Sonata and Toccata; the Toccata, by the way, is not included in the Breitkopf & Härtel edition; it appeared first, we believe, together with the sonata, in a London edition. Beethoven's first sonatas (Op. 2) appeared only in 1796).[1]   By 1802, Clementi had published up to Op. 40; in which year Beethoven composed two of the three sonatas, Op. 31, Nos. 1–3. Between 1820–21 appeared Clementi's sonata, Op. 46 (dedicated to Kalkbrenner), and the last set of three sonatas in (including the "Didone Abbandonata") Op. 50. Beethoven's sonata in E (Op. 109) appeared in November 1821. Thus Clementi at first influenced Beethoven, but, later on, the reverse must have been the case.

Breitkopf & Härtel have published sixty-four sonatas of Clementi; and of these, sixty-three are to be found in the Holle edition.[2]

The three sonatas, Op. 2, Nos. 1, 2, 3 (25, 26, 27), have only two movements, and are principally remarkable for their showy technique.[3]

---

[1] The three Sonatas in E flat, F minor, and D, dedicated to Maximilian Frederick, Elector of Cologne, and published at Speyer in 1783, are not here taken into account.

[2] In mentioning any of them we shall first give the Breitkopf & Härtel numbers and then the Holle numbers in brackets, so that either edition may be referred to.

[3] At the time of their production Dussek was not born, Hummel was still a child, and Beethoven an infant "mewling and puking in the nurse's arms," if, indeed, the Beethovens were able to afford the luxury of a nurse. Even Emanuel Bach had not published any of his Leipzig Collections, neither had Haydn written his best sonatas. As Clementi was not only the survivor of Beethoven, but also his predecessor, a reminder as to the state of the sonata world, when Clementi first entered it, is not wholly unnecessary.

Clementi, of course, was well acquainted with Scarlatti's music, yet it would perhaps be difficult to point out any direct influence of the one over the other.   In the next three sonatas, Op. 9, Nos. 4, 5, 6 (11, 28, 12), the first and third are most interesting.   In the second, Clementi indulges in his favourite passages of thirds, sixths, and octaves; there is, indeed, a Presto movement, a *moto perpetuo* for the right hand, in octaves, which, if taken up to time, would tax even pianists of the present day.   The 1st sonata may be noticed for its bold chords, and its *sforzandos* on unaccented beats, which sound Beethovenish.   The 3rd sonata reminds us in many ways of the Bonn master. In the opening Allegro there is a sighing figure—

which plays an important part throughout the movement, and therefore gives a marked character to it. In the development section the bold contrasts, the powerful chords, the sighing figure in augmentation, all point to Beethoven.   And, curiously enough, the principal theme, which now appears in major (the sonata is in G minor), reminds one very strongly of the " Eroica "—

It is worth noticing that the " sighing figure " may be traced in the other two movements of the

sonata.   The next sonata, No. 10 (44), has three
movements, all in the same key ; the Trio of the
Minuet is in the key of the subdominant.   In the
first movement may be noticed the extension of
a phrase by repetition (*pp*) of its last two notes,
a feature often to be met with in Beethoven
(see, for instance, the first movement of the
" Appassionata," development section).

The *piano* phrase in the Rondo of No. 11 (45),
before the organ point and the pause bar, is
striking.   No. 14 (2) is interesting.   The broken
octaves at the end of the exposition section, and
the return by ellipsis to the principal theme, call
to mind passages in Beethoven's Op. 22 and Op.
109.   Sonata No. 16 (4) has a delightful first
movement ; the evolution of the second subject
from the first deserves attention.   In No. 18 (51)
there is one point to notice.   The key of the first
movement is in F, but the principal theme in
the recapitulation section appears in E flat ; the
second theme, however, according to rule, in the
tonic.

Sonata No. 19 (52), in F minor, demands more
than a passing word.   Our readers will, perhaps,
be tired of our noticing foreshadowings of Beethoven, yet we must add others here.   We can
assure them, however, or rather those who are not
familiar with Clementi's sonatas, that the passages
to which we call attention only form a small proportion of those to which we might refer.   The
first movement (Allegro agitato) is concise ; there

is no padding.   Every bar of the exposition section
may be termed thematic.   The second subject, in
the orthodox relative major, is evolved from the
principal theme.   And the latter descends, but
the former ascends—a true Beethoven contrast.
The coda to the first section, with its working of
a thematic figure in augmentation, forms a striking
feature.   At the close of the development section
a long dignified dominant passage seems a pre-
paration for the return of the principal theme, but
the composer has a surprise ; after a pause bar, the
second theme appears, and in A flat.   A modulation soon leads back to F minor, and quite in Beethoven fashion—

and the exposition coda is repeated in extended
form.   In the next movement (Largo e sostenuto)
sombre tones still prevail ; the key is that of the
dominant minor.   There is evident kinship between the first and last movements ; of this the
opening bar of the former and the closing bars
of the latter offer signal proof.

In No. 23 (43) at the end of the last movement,
an organ point reminds us that the full intentions
of the composer are not recorded.   Thus, in
Clementi's early sonatas at any rate, the inter-

preter, as in E. Bach's works, was expected to make additions.   In No. 26 (7) the opening of the theme of the Arietta recalls, and in no vague manner, the opening of the Finale of Beethoven's Septet.   No. 34 (8) is an excellent sonata ; there is considerable freedom in the recapitulation section. In No. 39 (35) Clementi returns to an old form of sonata : there are only two movements, a Larghetto and Tempo di Minuetto, and both in the same key.   With sonata No. 41 (32), the first of two published as Op. 34, Clementi breaks new ground. The idea of incorporating the subject-matter of an introductory slow movement had already occurred to Haydn,[1] but Clementi goes to greater lengths. (It must not be forgotten that Beethoven's " Sonate Pathétique," Op. 13, appeared in 1799 ; possibly, before Clementi's.)   From the opening character-istic subject of the Largo is evolved the principal subject of the Allegro *con fuoco*, and there is also relationship between it and the second sub-ject.   In the unusually long development section, a dramatic passage, evolved from the concluding bars of the Largo, leads to a slow section in which the opening notes of the Largo are given out in loud tones, and in the unexpected key of C major (the three repeated *sforzando* crotchets remind one of the " fate " notes in the C minor Symphony) ; and when the Tempo primo is re-sumed, the

[1] London Symphony in E flat, No. 8 (No. 1 in Breitkopf & Härtel *Catalogue*).

also reminds one of

in the same movement of the above-mentioned
Symphony. Then, again, in an important coda
the theme is given out in modified, yet intensified
form. In the Finale of the sonata the Largo still
makes its influence felt. Exception may perhaps
be taken to the length of the first movement, and
to the prominence throughout the work, of the
principal key; but the evident desire of the composer to express something which was inwardly
moving him gives great interest to the music.

The sonata in B minor, Op. 40, is one of
Clementi's most finished productions. The name
of Beethoven must again be mentioned ; for depth
of meaning, boldness, style of development, and
gradation of interest, the music comes within
measurable distance of the greater master. Not
only is there no padding, but here the technique
serves a higher purpose than that of display ;
there are no formal successions of thirds, sixths,
or octaves, no empty bravoura passages. The long
development section of the first movement, with its
bold contrasts, its varied presentation of thematic
material, its peculiar mode of dealing with fragments of a theme, and its long dwelling on dominant

harmony previous to the return of the principal
theme,—all these things remind one of Beethoven.
This movement is followed by a Largo (*mesto
e patetico*) leading to the final Allegro.   These
two are intimately connected ; and, moreover, the
latter includes reminiscences from the introductory
Adagio.   After a brief reference to the Largo, the
movement concludes with a passionate Presto coda.
In Mr. Banister's *Life of Macfarren* we learn that
the latter considered the B minor of Clementi
" one of the finest sonatas ever written " ; and
many musicians will, probably, agree with him.

Of the three last sonatas (Op. 50, Nos. 1, 2, and
3), it must be remembered that when they appeared
Beethoven had published up to Op. 106, and
possibly Op. 109.   If, then, in some of the earlier
Clementi sonatas we spoke of his influence on
Beethoven, it is just the reverse here.   Nevertheless, of these sonatas which must have been known
to that master, one may have led him to think
again of the idea of revealing the poetic basis of
his sonatas.[1]   Clementi gives the title, " Didone
Abbandonata : Scena Tragica " to his work.   The
introductory Largo is *sostenuto e patetico*, while
the Allegro which follows bears the superscription,
deliberando e meditando ; the Adagio is *dolente* ;
and the Allegro Finale, *agitato e con disperazione*.
The music expresses throughout the sorrow and
despair of the forsaken queen, while certain
wild passages (as for example the coda of the

[1] See p. 187 concerning Beethoven's conversation with Schindler.

first Allegro) tell also of her anger. This Allegro is an admirably sustained movement, and, at moments, the composer rises to the height of his argument. It is interesting, too, from a technical point of view, for there is no empty display. Whatever degree of inspiration may be accorded to the music, it will surely be acknowledged that the composer was full of his theme ; that all his powers of head and heart were engaged in the task of illustration. This " Dido " sonata, of course, suffers if compared with those of Clementi's great contemporary ; and some of the writing is formal and old-fashioned, and, at times, too thin to attract the sympathy or to excite the interest of pianists of the present day, who enjoy the richer inheritance of Beethoven, the romantic tone-pictures of Schumann and Brahms, the fascinating miniatures of Chopin, and the clever glitter of Liszt. Still it does not deserve utter oblivion. Hear what Fr. Rochlitz says of it in the *Allg. Mus. Zeit. :* " It (the sonata) is indeed a tragic scene, one so clearly thought out and so definitely expressed, that it is by no means difficult —not only in each movement, but in its various divisions—to follow literally the course of changing feeling which is here developed."

Schindler, with regard to the work, also remarks as follows : " Who understands nowadays how to interpret this musical soul-picture (written unfortunately in old stereotyped sonata-form !) ? At best, glancing hastily over it, a pianist carelessly remarks that the poetical contents of this sonata are only expressed in the title." And again : "In the year 1827, at Baden, near Vienna, Clementi gave me details respecting the contents and interpretation of this tone-poem. A new edition of the work by J. André of Offenbach enabled me to insert a preface with the explanations of the veteran master."[1] And further, as a tone-picture expressing states of the soul, he knows " of no other work entitled sonata more worthy of a place beside those of Beethoven."

II. Johann Ludwig Dussek

This composer comes next to Clementi, in order of time, and, we may add, of merit. His natural gifts really exceeded those of Clementi; but the latter made a deep study of his art, and also of the pianoforte, to which, indeed, like Chopin, he devoted his whole attention. Dussek was fond of ease and pleasure, and never developed his powers to the full. It may be noted that both these celebrated pianists were connected with English music-publishing houses. Clementi prospered, though not in his first undertaking with Longman & Broderip; but Dussek was unsuccessful, and left England, so it is said, to avoid his creditors. There is, indeed, a letter written by Dussek from Hamburg, dated 12th June, 1801, to Clementi, and apart from the curious spectacle of these two pianists in commercial

[1] Schindler, *Biography of Beethoven*, 3rd ed. vol. ii. pp. 223-4.

correspondence with each other, the letter is of interest, in that it belongs to a period of Dussek's life concerning the details of which there is some uncertainty.[1]   Dussek, it may be mentioned, does

HAMBURGH, June 12, 1801.

[1] MR. CLEMENTI,
   MON CHER CLEMENTI,—

J'ai reçu avec un extrême plaisir votre lettre, aussi que *L'Autoscript* dans celle de ma femme, je suis extremement touché du désir que vous témoignez de me revoir à Londres, mais etant une fois dans le Continent je ne puis résister au désir de faire une visite à mon Père, d'autant plus qui je Lui ai déja écrit que je viendrai pour Sure le voir cette eteé, je sçais par Ses lettres qu'il attend ce moment comme la plus grande, et peut-être, la dernière jouissance de sa Vie ; tromper dans une pareille attente un Viellard de 70 ans, ce serait anticiper sur sa mort, d'ailleurs en arrivant en Angleterre tout de suite je ne ferais également que manger mon argent, ou bien celui de ma femme jusqu'à l'hiver prochain, aussi ma resolution est prise de faire le Voyage de la Boheme ; voire en passant Dresde, Prague et Vienne, ou je sçais que je puis gagner de quoi me defrayer de tout mon voyage, et au dela : et de revenir a Londres vers le Novembre, vous pouvez compter ladessus, mais surtout sur le plaisir que j'aurai de revoir et d'embrasser un ami tel que vous—Mardi prochain part d'ici pour Londres un commis de Mr. Parish *un des premiers Banquiers d'ici* qui vous remetra en mains propres, par un de vos associés, mes trois nouvelles Sonates,—je suis occupé a metre au net.   Les trois Concertinos qui vous recevrez aussi dans une quinzaine au plus tard, dont j'espere qui vous serez assez content, etant le meilleur ouvrage que j'ai jamais fait *in the Selling Way*, adieu mon cher Clementi, Les oreilles doivent souvent vous tinter, car je parle constamment de vous a tout le monde, car tout le monde aime qu'on leur parle de leurs connaissances, or vous êtes de la connaissance de tout le monde, adieu.

Votre ami,
DUSSEK.

MESSRS LONGMAN, CLEMENTI, & CO.,
   GENTELMEN AND FRIENDS,—
   I beg you would do your possible to send to me the two grand

not ever appear to have returned to London. In
1803 he became attached to Prince Louis
Ferdinand, to whom he offered advice in pianoforte playing and composition. There is another
letter extant of Dussek's written in the same year
in which that Prince fell on the battlefield of
Saalfeld (13th October, 1806), and this also we
will give, as we believe, like the one above, it has
never been published.[1]   The catalogue of Dussek's

instruments immediately, for the two Gentelmen whom I have
persuaded to purchase them after they have heard my own, are
very impatient about it, and I am afraid if I do not receive a
decided Answer from you about it or the *connoisement*, wich I may
Show them, they will be induced to Buy some of their German
Instruments as they are pretty well influenced by the Capel Master
of this Town who is a tolerable great As in Music and an
illnatured Antianglomane, besides I expect it as the means to make
my Journey to Bohemia, therefore I hope you will be so good, and
make the greatest Speed you can—you will see by the above that I
intend to be in London about November Next, when I will be very
happy to settle with you what may Balance in our account and to
continue faithfull to our agreement.

Believe me,
Gentelmen and Friends,
Yours faithfully,
DUSSEK.

You have no Idea how many proposals I have received from
London about my Compositions, some of them will make you
Laugh.

[1] AT THE GENERAL QUARTERS OF THE PRUSSIAN
ARMY IN SAXONY, *the 4th 8ber* 1806.

DEAR SIR,—
I have lately composed three Quartettos for two Violins, Tenor
and Violoncello, and confess to you that I think this work above all
that I have composed, they are neither in the Stile of Mozart, or
Haydn, nor that of Pleyel, they are in the Stile of Dussek and I

works, in Sir G. Grove's *Dictionary of Music and Musicians*, mentions three quartets for strings (Op. 60 : in G, B flat, and E flat), most probably the works referred to in the second letter.

Dussek, born in the year 1761, studied first with his father J. J. Dussek, and in his twenty-second year received further instruction from Emanuel Bach ; he soon enjoyed great fame as an executant. Tomaschek, himself a pianist of note, thus speaks of him in his autobiography :—

" There was, in fact, something magical about

will hope make some noise in the Musical World—the Price for the Propriety of them in Britain is 60 guineas, wich I think highly moderate considering the scarcity of good new Quartettos—I have particularly chosen you Sir for the publication of this work, because I allways found you very reasonable in the few Business I have had the pleasure to make with you, and as my Contract with Clementi & Co. finishes the 4th November this year, I should be very glad to continue with you the publication of all my Works in futur—These Quartettos are for you a publication so advantagous that I have not the least doubt but you will make the Bargain of them, since there is such a long time that nothing has been published of my composition—I wish them to appear about the middle of January, and to be dedicated *to His Royal Highness the Prince Louis of Prussia* with whom I am at this moment at the Army against the French—If you wish to write to me, give the letter to the Gentelmen who shall deliver to you the quartettos— —I beg You to give my best greetings to Mr. Crassier, Sheener, Tonkinson and all Those that remember me, and believe me,

Your very obedient Servant,
and sincere friend,
DUSSEK,
Privy Secretary to His Royal Hs.
the Prince Louis of Prussia.

The above letter is addressed to Mr. Birchal, Music Seller, New Bond Street, London.

the way in which Dussek, with all his charming grace of manner, through his wonderful touch, extorted from the instrument delicious and at the same time emphatic tones. His fingers were like a company of ten singers, endowed with equal executive powers, and able to produce with the utmost perfection whatever their director could require. I never saw the Prague public so enchanted as they were on this occasion by Dussek's splendid playing. His fine declamatory style, especially in *cantabile* phrases, stands as the ideal for every artistic performance—something which no other pianist has since reached."

The above quotation refers to a concert given at Prague in 1804.

There is, unfortunately, great confusion in the opus numbers of Dussek's works; and, moreover, it is difficult, if not impossible, to give the dates either of composition or publication. Breitkopf & Härtel have published more than fifty sonatas, but we shall only refer to some of the more important ones. Dussek, like all the prominent composers of his time, not even excepting Haydn and Mozart, wrote music on a practical, rather than on a poetical basis; one of the letters given above acknowledges this in very frank terms. But to Dussek's credit be it said, his least valuable works are masterpieces as compared with those which the sonata-makers, Steibelt, Cramer, and others, fabricated by the hundred. In Dussek we find great charm and refinement, while the writing

for the instrument is often highly attractive; but
the art of developing themes was certainly not his
strong point.   That he was at times careless or
indifferent may be seen from such a bar as the
following (Op. 47, No, 1, Litolff ed.; Adagio,
bar 9) :—

The bar before the return of the principal theme
in the Allegro of the sonata in E flat (Op. 75)
furnishes another instance.   Again, in the Allegro
of the sonata in A flat, known as " Le Retour à
Paris," there is a passage (commencing fifteen bars
before the end of the exposition section) which,
with slight alteration, might have been materially
improved.

Of the early sonatas, Op. 10, No. 2, in G minor,
is an interesting work.   It consists of two well-
contrasted movements : an Adagio in binary, and
a Vivace in sonata form.   Of the Presto of Op. 10,
No. 3, Professor Prout, in his interesting article,
Dussek's Pianoforte Sonatas,[1] says : " Both the first
and second principal subjects remind us irresistibly
of that composer (Mendelssohn), while the phrase at
the conclusion of the first part, repeated at the end
of the movement, is almost identical with a well-
known passage in the first movement of the

[1] *Musical Times*, September and October 1877.

' Scotch Symphony.' Is the coincidence acci-
dental, or did Mendelssohn know the sonata, and
was he unconsciously influenced by it ? "

In his three last sonatas (Op. 70, 75, and 77),
Dussek rises to a very high level; he was
undoubtedly influenced by the earnestness of
Beethoven, the chivalric spirit of Weber, and the
poetry of Schubert. A new era had set in. These
three composers were neither the *fools* of princes
nor the servants of the public : they were in the
world, yet not of it. They looked upon their art
as a sacred thing; and most probably the shallow-
ness of much of the music produced in such
abundance towards the close of the eighteenth
century spurred them on to higher efforts. Dussek
had lived an irregular, aimless sort of life; he had
wandered from one country to another, and had
acquired the ephemeral fame of the *virtuoso*. Perhaps he was a disappointed man ; there is a tinge
of sadness about these last sonatas which supports
such a view. Perhaps a feeling that his life was
ebbing away made him serious : his music now
shows no trifling. Explain it as you may, Dussek's
three last contributions to sonata literature rank
amongst the best of his day; and the indifference
now shown to them—so far, at least, as the concert
platform is concerned—is proof of ignorance, or
bad taste. We say ignorance, because the rising
generation has few, if any, opportunities of hearing
this composer's music. It is eighteen years since
his Op. 70 was given at the Popular Concerts;

while twenty-three and twenty-nine years have passed since Op. 75 and Op. 77 have been played there.

The sonata in A flat, entitled " Le Retour à Paris," is known in England as " Plus Ultra," and in an old edition it is dedicated to " Non plus Ultra." The latter was meant for Woelfl, a famous pianist and contemporary. His music is now forgotten, and his name is principally remembered in connection with Beethoven ; like the latter, his talent for improvisation was great. The late J. W. Davidson, in his long and interesting preface to Brewer & Co.'s edition of Dussek's A flat sonata, leads us to believe that Dussek's publisher, and not the composer himself, was responsible for the change of title to " Plus Ultra." The opus number, too, was changed from 70 to 71. The following story is also told by Davidson in a preface contributed by him to the Brewer edition of the Woelfl sonata :—" Who will play it ? " asked the publisher (Well), looking through the music of the composer. " I vill it blay," replied Woelfl. " Yes, but you won't buy the copies. No one but yourself or Dussek can play the Allegro, and I doubt if either of you can play the variations." Woelfl, however, sitting down before an old harpsichord, convinced the publisher of his error. "What shall we call it ? " asked Well. " Call it ' Ne plus Ultra,'" said Woelfl, rubbing his hands with joy, and adding, " Now shall we see if Herr von Esch vill more blay, or Herr Bomdembo make de variation."

Dussek's "Plus Ultra" (Op. 70) is justly admired;
the music is fine, and in the matter of technique,
setting aside a few sensational passages [1] in Woelfl's
sonata, which his very long fingers enabled him
to execute with comparative ease, far surpassed
the earlier work. It must appear strange to many
musicians who do not possess a copy of Woelfl's
sonata, that, in any mention of the rivalry between
the two composers, no reference is made to
Woelfl's sonata beyond the title. An examina-
tion of the latter, however, would soon solve the
mystery. The plain fact is this : both the music
and even the technique are now absolutely uninteresting. The sonata, in the key of F major,
commences with a brief introductory Adagio,
followed by a long, tedious Allegro abounding
in passages of thirds. A brief Andante comes
between this Allegro and the Finale, consisting
of flimsy variations on the popular melody " Life
let us Cherish." In a book of small compass such
as the present one, we only wish to dwell upon
matters of interest. For some particular purpose
Woelfl's sonatas might possibly prove of importance and even interest ; but not here. The " Non
plus Ultra," so far as we are concerned, may serve
to remind us that Woelfl once lived ; while the rest

[1] Here is one, in the 8th Variation—

Allegretto.

etc.

of his music, like some incidents in his life, may be consigned to oblivion. We cannot say that we have read all his sonatas, but enough of them, we believe, to judge, generally, of their contents.

Professor Macfarren's opinion of Dussek, as composer for the pianoforte, in the *Imperial Dictionary of Biography*, is so excellent, that we cannot perhaps do better than quote his words:—

" The immense amount of Dussek's compositions for the pianoforte have by no means equal merit; many of them were written for the mere object of sale, still more for the purpose of tuition, and some with the design of executive display. Of those which were produced, however, in the true spirit of art, expressing the composer's feelings in his own unrestrained ideas, there exist quite enough to stamp him one of the first composers for his instrument; and while these are indispensable in the complete library of the pianist, they are above value to the student in the development of his mechanism and the formation of his style. A strong characteristic of the composer is his almost redundant profusion of ideas;[1] but his rich fecundity of invention is greatly counterbalanced by diffuseness of design, resulting from the want of that power of condensation by means of which greater interest is often given to less beautiful matter."

And then, again, in an analysis of a Dussek Quintet, he remarks that in that composer's works

[1] Mendelssohn, too, complained that Dussek was a prodigal.

we may trace "not only the origin of many of the most beautiful effects with which later writers have been accredited, but some of the identical ideas by which these very writers have made their way into popularity."

III. Friedrich Wilhelm Rust

During the years 1744–45 a young man named Johann Ludwig Anton Rust went to Leipzig to study jurisprudence and philosophy.   But he was also musical, and played the violin at performances given under the direction of J. S. Bach.   On returning to his home at Wörlitz, Rust tried to inspire those around him with enthusiasm for the music of Bach.   With his younger brother, Friedrich Wilhelm, he was, at any rate, successful ; for the latter, already at the age of thirteen, was able to play by heart the whole of the "Well-tempered Clavier."   Later on, young Friedrich went to Halle to study law, and there not only made the acquaintance of Friedemann Bach, but, in return for attending to the correspondence of that gifted musician, he received from him instruction in composition, organ and clavier playing. Afterwards, at Potsdam, he continued his clavier studies under Emanuel Bach.   Surely a finer training never fell to the lot of any pupil.   Schumann recommends young musicians to make Bach their daily bread ; and of that, Rust must have had full weight.   But the list of his teachers is not yet exhausted ; he went to Italy in 1765, and studied the violin under Tartini. Rust composed operas, cantatas, concertos, and sonatas for violin,[1] and for pianoforte; the last-named, of which he wrote eight, now concern us.

The earliest, entitled "Sonata Erotica," was composed in 1775; this work, however, was not published until the year 1888 (edited by his grandson, Dr. Wilhelm Rust,[2] late cantor of St. Thomas'). It is the first of a series of works extraordinary in many ways—in form, subject-matter, developments, and technique. With regard to the last-named, there is something to say, and it had better be said at once. Dr. E. Prieger, in his interesting pamphlet, *F. W. Rust: Ein Vorgänger Beethovens*, remarks as follows:—
"While the grandson, full of enthusiasm, threw his whole soul into the creations of his ancestor, he gave a reflection, in his edition, of the pictures which had been vividly formed in his mind." To accomplish this he has strengthened the writing, and, in some cases, *modernised* it. Dr. Prieger, who has seen some, if not all of the autographs, has assured us that "these additions only concern the exterior, and do not affect the fundamental, character of the work." This statement is, to a certain extent, satisfactory, and we receive it thankfully. But a great deal of the writing is far ahead of the age in which it was written; it

[1] The one in D minor has often been performed at the Popular Concerts.

[2] 1822-1892.

reminds one now of Weber, now of Schumann. Why, one may ask, did not the editor indicate the additions in smaller notes? Then it would have been possible to see exactly what the elder Rust had written, and what the younger Rust had added. At present one can only marvel at some of the writing, and long to know how much of it really belongs to the composer. It appears that Rust, as editor of his grandfather's work, had some intention of describing his editions, etc., but death, which frequently prevents the best intentioned plans, intervened.

The "Sonata Erotica" is noticeable, generally, for its charm, poetry, and spontaneity. The first movement, an Allegro moderato, is in sonata-form. The second, in the key of the relative minor, entitled Fantasie, has in it more of the spirit of Beethoven than of Emanuel Bach. The Finale is in rondo form; the middle section consists of a playful Duettino, containing free imitations.

The next sonata (1777), in D flat, opens with a graceful Allegretto, and closes with a Tempo di Minuetto, which, for the most part, points backward rather than forward. The slow movement, Adagio sostenuto, is, however, of a higher order than either of these. It has Beethovenish breadth and dignity, yet lacks the power of the Bonn master: those magic touches by which the latter makes us feel his genius, and secures gradation of interest up to the very close of a movement. This Adagio, however, were the date of its composition unknown, might pass for a very clever imitation of Beethoven's style.

In 1784, Rust wrote two sonatas, one in F sharp minor, the other in B flat minor. The latter consists of three movements, and the music, especially in the Adagio in E flat minor, bears traces of the great Bach; still there are passages which sound more modern even in this very Adagio, which points so clearly to him as the source of inspiration. The modern element, however, admits of explanation, for Haydn and Mozart, at the time in which the sonata was written, had appeared in the musical firmament. But in the works we are about to mention, the composer suggests Beethoven, Weber, and even Schumann. In writing about Clementi, we were compelled frequently, and at the risk of wearying our readers, to call attention to foreshadowings of both the letter and spirit of Beethoven. The cases of Clementi and Rust, however, are not quite parallel. With the former it was mere foreshadowing; with exception of a few passages in which there was note resemblance between the two composers, the music still bore traces of Clementi's mode of thought and style of writing. But with Rust, there are moments in which it is really difficult to believe that the music belongs to a pre-Beethoven period.

The sonata [1] in D minor (1788) opens with a vigorous yet dignified Allegro; the graceful Adagio

[1] The original title is: "Sonata per il Cembalo ò Fortepiano di F. W. Rust, 1788."

is of eighteenth century type; it is in the key of
the relative major, but closes on the dominant
chord of D minor, leading without break to a final
Allegro, full of interesting details. The movement
concludes with an impressive *poco adagio* coda, in
which Rust makes use of the principal theme of
the opening movement. We will venture on one
quotation, although a few bars, separated from the
context, may convey only a feeble impression—

The sonata in D major, composed six years
later, opens with an interesting Allegro. The
second movement, in B minor, bears the superscription "Wehklage" (Lamentation). Rust's
eldest son, a talented youth, who was studying

at Halle University, was drowned in the river Saale, 23rd March 1794. Matthisson, the "Adelaide" poet, sent to the disconsolate father a poem entitled "Todtenkranz für ein Kind," to which Rust sketched music, and on that sketch is based this pathetic movement, which sounds like some tone-poem of the nineteenth century. Here is the impressive coda:—

There follows a dainty, old-fashioned Minuet, and a curious movement entitled "Schwermuth und Frohsinn" (Melancholy and Mirth);[1] though after the "Wehklage" these make little impression.

During four years (1792–96), Rust was occupied with a sonata in C minor and major. The work is a remarkable one. It opens with an energetic Recitativo in C minor, interrupted for a few bars by an Arioso Adagio in C major. Then comes a Lento in six-four time based on the celebrated Marlbrook song, a dignified movement containing, among other canonic imitations, one in the ninth. It leads by means of a *stringendo* bar to a brilliant Allegro con brio, a movement of which both the music and the technique remind one of Beethoven's bravoura style. A second section of the sonata commences with the recitative phrase of the opening of the work, only in A minor. This leads to a highly characteristic Andante, which Dr. Rust, the editor, in a preface to the published sonata, likens to the "mighty procession" in Lenau's *Faust*. The Finale consists of an animated Allegro, with a clever fugato by way of episode; there is still an Allegro maestoso, which, except for its length and the fact that it contains a middle section, Cantabile e religioso, we should call a long coda. The whole, evidently programme-

---

[1] It is curious to note that in the supplement of the Breitkopf & Härtel edition of Beethoven's works there are two little pieces entitled "Lustig und Traurig."

music, is a sonata worked out somewhat on Kuhnau lines.

Now, was Beethoven acquainted with Rust's music ? Dr. Prieger, in the pamphlet mentioned above, remarks as follows :—" During the years 1807–27 Wilhelm Karl Rust (*b.* 1787, *d.* 1855), the youngest son of our master, was in Vienna, and had the good fortune to make the acquaint-ance of Beethoven, who was pleased with his playing, and recommended him as teacher. Among Rust's lady pupils were Baroness Doro-thea Ertmann and Maximiliane Brentano, both of whom belonged to Beethoven's most intimate circle of friends, and had been honoured by having works dedicated to them. The younger Rust was gifted with an extraordinary memory, and therefore it seems more than probable that he occasionally performed some of his father's works in that circle. On the other hand, we have Beet-hoven's energetic nature holding aloof from any-thing which might influence his own individuality."

There, in a few words, is the answer to our question. And it is about the only one we can ever hope to obtain. Rust was altogether a remarkable phenomenon, a musician born, as it were, out of due time. If Beethoven, as seems quite possible, was acquainted with his music, then Rust exerted an influence over the master quite equal to that of Clementi. It almost seems as if we ought to say, greater.

CHAPTER VII

LUDWIG VAN BEETHOVEN

BACH'S forty-eight Preludes and Fugues and Beethoven's thirty-two Sonatas tower above all other works written for the pianoforte ; they were aptly described by the late Dr. Hans v. Bülow, the one as the Old, the other as the New Testament of musical literature. Each fresh study of them reveals new points of interest, new beauties ; they are rich mines which it is impossible to exhaust. Bach seemed to have revealed all the possibilities of fugue-form ; and the history of the last seventy years almost leads one to imagine that Beethoven was the last of the great sonata writers. To this matter, however, we will presently return. In speaking of the various composers from Kuhnau onwards, we have tried to show the special, also the earliest, influences acting on them ; and we shall still pursue the same course with regard to Beethoven. When he went to Vienna in 1792 he found himself in the very centre of the musical world. Haydn, though past sixty years of age, was at the zenith of his fame ; and Beethoven, for a time, studied under him. Mozart had died in

160

the previous year, so his name was still in every-body's mouth. The early works of Beethoven give strong evidence of the influence exerted over him by these two composers. Then Prince Lich-nowsky, the friend and pupil of Mozart, and Baron van Swieten, the patron and friend of both Haydn and Mozart, were among the earliest to take notice of the rising genius and to invite him to their musical *matinées* and *soirées*; and one can easily guess what kind of music was performed on those occasions. But the little story of Beethoven remaining at van Swieten's house, after the guests had departed, in order to " send his host to bed with half a dozen of Bach's Fugues by way of *Abendsegen*," reminds us of another strong, and still earlier, influence. At Bonn, under the guidance of his master, Christian Gottlob Neefe, Beethoven was so well-grounded in the " Well-tempered Clavier," that already, at the age of twelve, he could play nearly the whole of it. But, if we are not mistaken, he also made early acquaintanceship with the sonatas of Emanuel Bach. For in 1773 Neefe published " Zwölf Klavier-Sonaten," which were dedicated to the composer just named. In the preface he says : "Since the period in which you, dearest Herr Capellmeister, presented to the public your masterly sonatas, worked out, too, with true taste, scarcely anything of a character-istic nature has appeared for this instrument.[1]

[1] E. Bach published six easy clavier sonatas in 1766, but Neefe probably refers to earlier and more important works.

Most composers have been occupied in writing
Symphonies, Trios, Quartets, etc. And if now
and then they have turned their attention to the
clavier, the greater number of the pieces have been
provided with an accompaniment, often of an
extremely arbitrary kind, for the violin ; so that
they are as suitable for any other instrument as
for the clavier." Then, later on, Neefe acknowledges how much instruction and how much
pleasure he has received from the theoretical and
practical works of E. Bach (we seem to be reading
over again the terms in which Haydn expressed
himself towards Bach). May we, then, not conclude that young Beethoven's attention was
attracted to these " masterly sonatas," and also
to those of his teacher Neefe? This is scarcely
the moment to describe the Neefe sonatas.[1] In
connection, however, with Beethoven, one or two
points must be noticed. In the third of the three
sonatas which Beethoven composed at the age of
eleven, the last movement is entitled : Scherzando
allegro ma non troppo, and twice in Neefe
do we come across the heading, Allegro e
scherzando (first set, No. 5, last movement ; and
second set, No. 1, also last movement). Then,
again, No. 2 of the second set opens with a brief
introductory Adagio, one, by the way, to some extent connected with the Allegro which follows.

---

[1] Besides those mentioned, he published in 1774 six new
sonatas, also variations on the theme "Kunz fand einst einen
armen Mann."

In the 2nd of the above-mentioned Beethoven
sonatas (the one in F minor) there is also a slow
introduction ; the young master, no mere imitator,
anticipates his own " Sonate Pathétique,"and repeats
it in the body of the Allegro movement.   Lastly,
no one, we believe, can compare the Neefe variations with those of Beethoven in the 3rd sonata
(in A) without coming to the conclusion that the
pupil had diligently studied his teacher's compositions, which, we may add, were thoroughly
sound, full of pleasing *cantabile* writing, and, at
times, not lacking in boldness.   Let us venture on
one quotation of only four bars from Sonata 1, in
G, of the second set of six : it is the opening of
a short Adagio connecting the Allegro with an
Allegro e scherzando—

The enharmonic modulation from the second
to the third bar reminds one of E. Bach, who
was so fond of such changes ; also of a similar
one in the " Pathétique."

Beethoven wrote thirty-two sonatas, and in the following table the opus number of each work is given, also the date of its publication; some have a title, and the greater number a dedication :—

Sonata		Published	Dedicated to
Op. 2	No. 1 (F minor)	1796.	Haydn.
„	No. 2 (A)	„	„
„	No. 3 (C)	„	„
Op. 7	(E flat)	1797.	Countess Babette Keglevics.
Op. 10	No. 1 (C minor)	1798.	Countess Browne.
„	No. 2 (F)	„	„
„	No. 3 (D)	„	„
Op. 13	(C minor, "Sonate Pathétique")	1799.	Prince Charles Lichnowsky.
Op. 14	No. 1 (E)	„	Baroness Braun.
„	No. 2 (G)	„	„
Op. 22	(B flat)	1802.	Count Browne.
Op. 26	(A flat)	„	Prince Charles Lichnowsky.
Op. 27	No. 1 (E flat)	„	Princess Liechtenstein.
„	No. 2 (C sharp minor)	„	Countess Giulietta Guicciardi.
Op. 28	(D)	„	Joseph de Sonnenfels.
Op. 31	No. 1 (G)	1803.	
„	No. 2 (D minor)	„	
„	No. 3 (E flat)	1804.	
Op. 49	No. 1 (G minor)	1805.	
„	No. 2 (G)	„	
Op. 53	(C)	„	Count Waldstein.
Op. 54	(F)	1806.	
Op. 57	(F minor)	1807.	Count Brunswick.
Op. 78	(F sharp)	1810.	Countess Theresa of Brunswick.
Op. 79	(G)	„	

Sonata		Published	Dedicated to
Op. 81A	(E flat; "Das Lebewohl, die Abwesenheit, das Wiedersehn")	1811.	Archduke Rudolph.
Op. 90	(E minor)	1815.	Count Moritz Lichnowsky.
Op. 101	(A)	1817.	Baroness Dorothea Ertmann.
Op. 106	(B flat)	1819.	Archduke Rudolph.
Op. 109	(E)	1821.	Maximiliane Brentano
Op. 110	(A flat)	1822.	
Op. 111	(C minor)	1823.	Archduke Rudolph.

The autograph of the last sonata does not bear any dedication, but, from a letter of Beethoven (1st June, 1823) to the Archduke, it is evident that it was intended for the latter.[1]

The fanciful name of "Moonlight" to Op. 27 (No. 2), the appropriate publisher's title of Op. 57, and the poetical superscriptions of Op. 81A, have, without doubt, helped those sonatas towards their popularity. It does not always happen that the most popular works of a man are his best; but these in question justly rank among Beethoven's finest productions. The last five sonatas are wonderful tone-poems; yet, with the exception, perhaps, of Op. 110, in A flat, as regards perfection of form and unity of conception, not one equals Op. 27 (No. 2), Op. 31 (No. 2), and Op. 57. Apart from any æsthetic considerations, the digital difficulties

---

[1] "As your Royal Highness seemed to be pleased with the sonata in C minor, I thought it would not appear too bold to surprise you with the dedication of it."

of the last five sonatas prevent their becoming common property.   The brilliant technique of Op. 53 has proved a special attraction to pianists, and it has therefore become widely known.   With this one sonata Beethoven proved his superiority, even in the matter of virtuosity, over the best pianists of his day.

In order to be able to enter fully into the spirit of the music of great composers, it is necessary to know the history of their lives.   Beethoven's is fairly well known.   But it may be worth while to refer, briefly, to the principal men and women to whom the master dedicated his pianoforte sonatas.

Of the thirty-two, as will be seen from the above table, eight have no dedication.

In the year 1792 Beethoven left Bonn and went to Vienna.   There he studied counterpoint under Haydn, yet the lessons proved unsatisfactory. But the fame and influence of the veteran master no doubt prompted the young artist to dedicate to him the three sonatas, Op. 2.   The title-page of the oldest Vienna edition runs thus :—

Trois Sonates pour le Clavecin Piano-forte composeés
et dedieés
A Mr. Joseph Haydn Docteur en musique par
Louis van Beethoven.

There was perhaps more of sarcasm than respect in the " Docteur en musique "; Beethoven is related to have said that he had taken some lessons from Haydn, but had never learnt anything from him.   Nevertheless he paid heed to

his teacher's music.   There are in the sonatas
one or two reminiscences of Haydn, which seem
to us curious enough to merit quotation.   One
occurs in the sonata in C minor (Op. 10, No. 1).
We give the passage (transposed) from Haydn, and
the one from Beethoven :—

"Letter V," Pohl, No. 58.[1]   HAYDN.

Op. 10, No. 1.   BEETHOVEN.

And another—

"In Native Worth" (*Creation*).   HAYDN.

Op. 31, No. 1.   BEETHOVEN.

[1] The opening theme of that same symphony—

While speaking of reminiscences, a curious one may be mentioned. The theme of the slow movement of Beethoven's sonata in A (Op. 2, No. 2) strongly resembles the theme of the slow movement of his own Trio in B flat (Op. 97):—

In Op. 111, again, the second subject of the Allegro recalls a phrase in the Presto of the Sonata in C sharp minor.

Haydn, as the most illustrious composer of that day, stands first; but the next name worthy of mention is Count Waldstein, a young nobleman who had been a guide, philosopher, and friend to Beethoven during the Bonn days. The well-known entry in the young musician's Album just before his departure for Vienna shows in what high esteem he was held by Waldstein. Count Ferdinand Waldstein died in 1823.

Prince Charles Lichnowsky was one of the composer's earliest patrons after the latter had settled in Vienna. The Prince, descended from

recalls, curiously, the last movement of Beethoven's 8th Symphony; and still more so in the form in which he first sketched it—

an old Polish family, was born in 1758, and, consequently, was, by twelve years, Beethoven's senior. He lived mostly in Vienna. In 1789 he invited Mozart to accompany him to Berlin; and the King's proposal to name the latter his capellmeister is supposed to have been suggested by the Prince. Lichnowsky was also a pupil of Mozart's. His wife, Princess of Thun, was famous for her beauty, her kindly disposition, and for her skill as a musician. Beethoven had not been twelve months in Vienna when he was offered rooms in the Prince's house. It was there that the pianoforte sonatas Op. 2 were first played by their author in presence of Haydn. Beethoven remained in this house until 1800. In 1799 the "Sonate Pathétique" was dedicated to the Prince, and in the following year the latter settled on him a yearly pension of 600 florins. In the year 1806 there was a rupture between the two friends. At the time of the battle of Jena, Beethoven was at the seat of Prince Lichnowsky at Troppau, in Silesia, where some French officers were quartered. The independent artist refused to play to them, and when the Prince pressed the request, Beethoven got angry, started the same evening for Vienna, and,—anger still burning in his breast,—on his arrival home, he shattered a bust of his patron. The composer's refusal to play to the French officers was grounded on his hatred to Napoleon, who had just won the battle of Jena. Beethoven, however, became reconciled with the Prince before the death of the latter in 1814. It should be mentioned that Beethoven's first published work, the three pianoforte Trios, was dedicated to Prince Lichnowsky.

The Archduke Rudolph (1788–1831) was one of the master's warmest friends, and one of his most devoted admirers.   His uncle was Max Franz, Elector of Cologne, to whose chapel both Beethoven and his father had belonged.   The Archduke was the son of Leopold of Tuscany and Maria Louisa of Spain; his aunt was Marie Antoinette, and his grandmother the famous Maria Theresa.   He is supposed to have made the acqaintance of Beethoven during the winter of 1803–4, and then to have become his pupil.   The pianoforte part of the Triple Concerto (Op. 58), commenced in 1804, and published in 1807, is said to have been written for him.

Concerning the Countess Giulietta Guicciardi, for whom Beethoven entertained a hopeless passion, and the Countess Theresa of Brunswick, to whom he is said to have been secretly engaged for some years, there is no necessity to enter into detail. Everyone has probably heard of the famous love-letters, and of the discussion as to which of these two they were addressed.   Maximiliane Brentano was a niece of the famous Bettine Brentano.

The Baroness Ertmann was an excellent performer on the pianoforte, and is said to have been unrivalled as an interpreter of Beethoven's music. Mendelssohn met her at Rome in 1831, and in a letter describes her playing of the C sharp minor and D minor Sonatas.

We must now turn to the sonatas, yet neither for the purpose of analysis nor of admiration. We shall briefly discuss how far Beethoven worked on the lines established by his predecessors, and how far he modified them. And, naturally, the question of music on a poetic basis will be touched upon.

The number of movements of which Beethoven's sonatas consist varies considerably : some have two, some three, others four. The three very early sonatas dedicated to Maximilian, Archbishop of Cologne, have only three movements (the second opens with a brief Larghetto, which, how-ever, really forms part of the first movement). But the four Sonatas Op. 2 (Nos. 1, 2 and 3) and Op. 7 all have four movements—an Allegro, a slow movement, a Scherzo or Minuet and Trio, and a final Allegro or Rondo. There are examples in later sonatas of similar grouping ; but it is an undeniable fact that in some of his greatest sonatas—Op. 31 (No. 2), Op. 27 (No. 2), Op. 53, Op. 57—he reverts to the three-movement sonata so faithfully adhered to by Emanuel Bach, Haydn, Mozart, and Clementi. And there is evidence that the omission of the Minuet or Scherzo in Op. 10 (Nos. 1 and 2), in Op. 13, and in others named above, was the result of reflection and not caprice.

Among sketches for the Sonatas, Op. 10,

Beethoven writes: "Zu den neuen Sonaten ganz
kürze Menuetten" (to the new sonatas quite short
Minuets); and also, a little further on, "Die
Menuetten zu den Sonaten ins künftige nicht
länger als von 16 bis 24 Takte" (in future
the Minuets to the sonatas not to exceed from
16 to 24 bars). Then, again, there are two
sketches for a movement of the Minuet or Scherzo
kind, which were almost certainly intended for
the Sonata No. 1 in C minor. One of these was
afterwards completed, and has been published
in the Supplement to Breitkopf & Härtel's
edition of Beethoven's works. Both these were
finally rejected, yet Beethoven made still another
attempt. There is a sketch for an "Intermezzo zur
Sonate aus C moll," and at the end of the music
the composer writes: "durchaus so ohne Trio,
nur ein Stück" (exactly thus without Trio, only
one piece). So the Minuets were to be short; then
the limit of length is prescribed; and, lastly, an
Intermezzo *without* Trio is planned. The composer proposed, but his δαίμων disposed; the
Sonata in C minor finally appeared in print with
only an Adagio between the two quick movements.

Schindler, in reference to the proposal made by
Hoffmeister to Beethoven to edit a new edition of
his pianoforte works, tells us that had that pro-
ject been carried out, the master, in order to get a
nearer approach to unity, would have reduced
some of his earlier sonatas from four movements
to three. And he adds: "He would most

certainly have cut out the Scherzo Allegro from the highly pathetic sonata for Pianoforte and Violin (Op. 30, No. 2; the first and third have only three movements), a movement in complete opposition to the character of the whole. He always objected to this movement, and, for the reason just assigned, advised that it should be omitted. Had the scheme been carried out, a small number of Scherzos, Allegros and Menuets would have been 'dismissed.' In our circle, however, objections were raised against this proposal; for among these Scherzos, etc., each of us had his favourite, and did not like the idea of its being removed from the place which it had long occupied. The master, however, pointed to the three-movement sonatas—Op. 10 in C minor, Op. 13, Op. 14, Op. 31 (Nos. 1 and 2), Op. 57, and others. The last sonatas—Op. 106 and Op. 110—which contain more than three movements must be judged in quite a different manner" (*Life of Beethoven*, 3rd ed. vol. ii. pp. 215–16).

Schindler's statements have sometimes been called in question; the above, however, bears on it the stamp of truth.

But how came it to pass that Beethoven's first four sonatas—Op. 2 (Nos. 1, 2, and 3) and Op. 7—have four movements? That is a question easier to ask than to answer. Schindler's remark that he followed custom is difficult to understand. In our introductory chapter we spoke of twenty sonatas containing four movements written

probably about the middle of the eighteenth
century, also of one of Wagenseil's for clavier
with violin accompanient; yet among the known
sonatas of that period, these form a minority.
Woelfl's Sonata in B flat (Op. 15) has four movements: Allegro, Andante, Scherzo Allegro, and
Finale (theme and variations), but that work
appeared shortly after Beethoven's Op. 2.

Even Haydn, who is said to have introduced
the Minuet into the Symphony, remained faithful
to the three-movement form of sonata.   Beethoven, however, wrote six sonatas consisting of
two movements. This change in the direction
of simplicity is striking, for in his quartets the
composer became more and more complex.   It
seems as if he were merely intent on exhibiting
strong contrast of mood: agitation and repose,
or fierce passion followed by heavenly calm; we
are referring especially to the Sonata in E minor
(Op. 90) and to the one in C minor (Op. 111).
The two sonatas of Op. 49—really sonatinas
written for educational purposes—may be dismissed;
also Op. 54, in the composition of which the head
rather than the heart of the master was engaged.
Even Op. 78, in F sharp, in spite of the Countess
of Brunswick, to whom it was dedicated, does not
seem the outcome of strong emotion; and therefore we do not take it now into consideration.
The two sonatas (Op. 90 and 111) mentioned above
are strong tone-poems, and the master having
apparently said all that he had to say, stopped.

The story, already related, about having no time to complete Op. 111 must not be taken seriously. Nevertheless, we do not for one moment imagine that Beethoven was thus reducing the number of movements in accordance with some preconceived scheme.

The D minor (Op. 31, No. 2) and the F minor (Op. 57) sonatas, not to speak of others, form the apotheosis of the sonata in three movements as established, though not invented, by Emanuel Bach.   To say that Beethoven was the perfecter of the sonata is true, but it is scarcely the whole truth.   The E minor appears a first great step in the process of dissolution ; the C minor, a second. They were great steps, because they were those of a very great man.   The experiments as to number of movements of which we spoke in our introductory chapter were interesting ; and with regard to the number, and also the position of the Minuet before or after the slow movement, those experiments acquired additional interest, inasmuch as Beethoven seems for a time to have been affected by them.   The two works named are, however, of the highest importance ; in them, if we are not mistaken, are to be found the first signs of the disappearance, as it were, of the sonata of three movements, and, perhaps, of the sonata itself, into the " imperceptible."   After Op. 90 Beethoven wrote sonatas in four movements, but that does not affect the argument, neither does the fact, that after Beethoven are to be found several remarkable sonatas with the same number. The process of evolution of the sonata was gradual; so also will be that of its dissolution. The title of " sonata " given by Beethoven to his Op. 90 and Op. 111 does not affect the music one jot; under any other name it would sound as well. You might call the " Choral Symphony " a Divertimento, and the title would be considered inappropriate; or a Polonaise, and the name would be scouted as ridiculous; but the music would still remain great and glorious. Yet taking into consideration the meaning of the term " sonata " as understood by Emanuel Bach, Haydn, and Beethoven himself, it can scarcely be the right one for these tone-poems in two sections. The sonata-form of the first movement in each case may have suggested the title. The two early sonatas Op. 27 (Nos. 1 and 2) are both styled sonata, but with the addition *quasi una fantasia*. And in neither case was the first movement in sonata-form; the one in E flat does not even contain such a movement. There are other signs of the process of disintegration in the later sonatas. Op. 109, in E, is peculiar as regards the form of the movements of which it is composed; and the fugues of Op. 101, 106, and 109—a return, by the way, to the past—show at least an unsettled state of mind. The sonata in A flat (Op. 110) was probably the germ whence sprang the sonata in B minor of Liszt—a work of which we shall soon have to speak.

Beethoven departed from the custom of his predecessors Haydn and Mozart, and the general practice of sonata-writers before him, in the matter of tonality.   In a movement in sonata-form the rule was for the second subject to be in the dominant key in the exposition section, and in the tonic in the recapitulation section, if the key of the piece was major; but if minor, in the relative major or dominant minor in the exposition, and in the tonic major or minor in the recapitulation.   Thus, if the key were C major, the second subject would be first in G major, afterwards in C major; if the key were C minor, first in E flat major, or G minor, afterwards in C minor or major.   In a minor movement the second subject is found more often in the relative major than in the dominant minor. The first and third movements of Beethoven's Sonata in D minor (Op. 31, No. 2) illustrate the latter; in each case the second subject is in A minor.

In major keys, besides that of the dominant, Beethoven chose the mediant (E) in his sonata in C (Op. 53); and in the recapitulation it occurs first in the sub-mediant (A), and only afterwards, in varied form, in the orthodox tonic.   Then in the B flat sonata (Op. 106) the second subject occurs in the sub-mediant (G).   In the last sonata in C minor, the second subject is neither in the relative major, nor in the dominant minor, but in the major key of the sub-mediant.   Once again, in the sonata in D major (Op. 10, No. 3) a second theme is introduced in the key of the relative minor before the dominant section is reached. With regard, indeed, to the number of themes and order of keys, some other movements of the Beethoven sonatas show departures from the orthodox rules.

In the important matter of the repeat of the first section of a movement in sonata-form, we find the master, for the most part, adhering to the custom delivered unto him by his predecessors. And yet there were two strong reasons why he might have been tempted to depart from it. The repetition was a survival from the old dance movements in binary form. E. Bach, Haydn, and Mozart not only repeated, but introduced various kinds of ornaments, and even harmonic changes ; and they expected performers to do the same. Beethoven, however, allowed no such licence—one, indeed, which in the hands of ordinary pianists would be calculated to spoil rather than to improve the music. Part, then, of the *raison d'être* of the repeat ceased to exist. But a still stronger temptation to suppress it must have been the *programme* or *picture* which Beethoven had in his mind when he composed. The repeat, now become almost an empty form, must have proved at times a fetter to his imagination. In many ways he was bold ; but in this matter strangely conservative. It was only in the sonata in F minor, Op. 57, that he first ventured to omit the repeat. It is not to be found in the opening movements of Op. 90 or Op 110, yet in his last sonata (Op. 111) the composer almost seems as if he wished to atone for his previous sins of omission. He had evidently not settled the question one way or the other ; but the fact that in three of his most poetical works he departed from custom, deserves note. Before his time the repeat, like the laws of the Medes and Persians, seemed irrevocably fixed.

Beethoven added important introductions or codas, or even both, to some of the movements of his sonatas. Codas are to be found in the sonatas both of Haydn and Mozart, but not introductory movements ; the idea of the latter, however, did not originate with Beethoven. The Grave which opens the " Pathétique " (Op. 13) does not merely throw the listener into the right mood for the Allegro, but the opening phrase—

is afterwards made use of in the development section—

and, later on, it occurs in double augmentation.

The *maestoso* which ushers in the Allegro of the last sonata contains foreshadowings which are better felt than explained.

At times the codas of Haydn are interesting, —as, for example, the one at the end of the first

movement of his "Genziger" Sonata in E flat,
—yet they do not present the thematic material
in any new or striking light.   With Beethoven it
is different.   In the Sonata in E flat (Op. 7) not
only is there contrapuntal working, but the principal theme, just at the close, is, as it were, rounded
off, completed.   Similar treatment may be seen
in the first movement of the Sonata in D (Op. 10,
No. 3) (here the effect is intensified by contrary
motion); also in the Allegro of Op 13, and other
sonatas; the opening movement of Op. 57 offers
a striking illustration.

The coda to the first movement of the "Waldstein" Sonata (Op. 53) is on a most elaborate
scale: it is almost as long as the development
section.   In the latter, only fragments of the
principal theme had been worked, but in the coda
it appears in complete form; fierce chords seem to
retard its progress, and a sinking, syncopated figure
is opposed to it, counteracting its rising, expanding
nature.   But it works its way onward and up-
ward, until, as if exhausted by the effort, two
descending scales lead to a quiet delivery of the
second theme, which had not been heard during
the development section.   Then principal theme
is given for the last time; it has overcome all
obstacles, and proclaims its victory in loud and
powerful chords.   The Presto which closes the
"Appassionata" (Op. 57) is one of Beethoven's
grandest codas, and all the more wonderful in that
it follows a movement of intense storm and stress.

It is a coda, not merely to the last movement, but to the whole work : it recalls the first, as well as the third movement.   The coda of the first move-ment of the C minor Symphony displays similar intensity ; there, however, we have an expression of strong will ; here, one of savage despair.   The coda of the first movement of the " Adieux " Sonata (Op. 81A) is another memorable ending.   The farewell notes sound sad in the opening Adagio, while in the Allegro which follows they are again plaintive, or else agitated.   But in the coda, though still sad, they express a certain tenderness, and the lingering of friends loth to part.   What-ever the special meaning of the music, the point which we here wish to emphasise is, that the coda presents thematic material, already amply developed, in quite a new light.

In the matter of structure, Beethoven may be said, in the main, to have followed Haydn and Mozart, but the effect of his music is, nevertheless, very different.   By overlapping of phrases; by very moderate use of full closes; by making passages of transition thoroughly thematic ; by affinity and yet strong contrast between his principal and second themes ; by a more organic system of development; by these and other means Beethoven surpassed his predecessors in power of continuity, intensity, and unity.   Then, again, his conception of tonality was broader, and his harmonies were more varied ; the fuller, richer tone of the piano-forte of his day influenced the character of his melodies; while the consequent progress of technique, as exhibited in the works of some of his immediate predecessors and contemporaries, enabled him to present his thoughts with greater variety and more striking effect than was possible to either Haydn or Mozart.

Once more, Beethoven seemed to be elaborating some central thought; Haydn and Mozart (with few exceptions), to be deftly weaving together thoughts so as to obtain pleasing contrasts. In a similar manner, the first and last movements of a sonata with Beethoven are of kindred mood, though perhaps of different degree. Haydn and Mozart seem again to be aiming at contrast; after a dignified opening Allegro and a soft, graceful slow movement, they frequently wind up with a Finale of which the chief characteristics are humour, playfulness, and merriment, so that the listener may part company from them in a pleasant frame of mind.

We have been comparing the composer, and to his advantage, with Haydn and Mozart. But the latter, however, sometimes come within near reach of the former; and had the means at their disposal been similar, they might possibly have equalled him. And, on the other hand, Beethoven's inspiration was sometimes at a comparatively low ebb. Speaking generally, however, the comparison, we believe, stands good.

John Sebastian Bach devoted the greater part of his life to the art of developing themes. His skill was wonderful, and so, too,—considering the restrictions of the fugue-form,—was the imagination which he displayed. In Beethoven the old master seems to live again, only under new and more favourable conditions. Bach was brought up in the way of the fugue, Beethoven of the sonata ; and, it may be added, from these, respectively, neither ever departed. From early youth onward, our composer was a deep student of Bach, and assimilated some of his predecessor's methods. One special feature of Beethoven's mode of development was to take a few notes, or sometimes merely a figure, from his theme, and to expand them into a phrase ; as, for instance, in the opening movement of the sonata in C minor (Op. 10, No. 1), in which

forms the material for the closing phrase of the exposition section. And the opening figure of the Finale of the same sonata is employed in a similar manner at the commencement of the second section of the movement. The Rondo of Op. 10, No. 3, furnishes good illustrations. Now let us turn to Bach. In the 13th Fugue of the "Well-tempered Clavier," the closing notes of the subject

are expanded, commencing at bar twenty-four,

into a melodious phrase.   Also in the Prelude which
follows (No. 14)

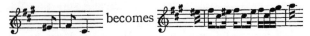

And some magnificent examples might be culled
from the noble Preludes in E flat and B flat minor
(Book 1, Nos. 8 and 22).   Again, another special
feature of Beethoven is the extension of a phrase
by repetition of the last clause,—a method too
familiar to need quotation.   But let us give one
illustration from Bach (Book 1, Fugue 6)—

The 8th Prelude of Book 1 has been already
mentioned to illustrate one point, but there are
other Beethovenisms in it.

   These comparisons must not be misunderstood ;
study of Bach strengthened Beethoven's genius.
We are not speaking of bald imitation, not even
of conscious imitation.   He not only received the
message of the old master, as a child, but while
he was a child ; and that no doubt helped him
more than all the works of his predecessors from
Emanuel Bach upwards.   It appealed to him
strongly, because it was based on nature.   Bach's
Fugues are living organisms ; they are expansions
of some central thought.   Development reveals
the latent power, the latent meaning of the
themes ; were it merely artificial, no matter how

skilful, it would be letter, not spirit. A clever contrapuntist once conceived the bold idea of competing with Bach; he wrote a series of Preludes and Fugues in all the keys, and displayed wonderful skill in all the arts of counterpoint, canon, and fugue, while in the matter of elaborate combinations he actually surpassed Bach (we refer here only to the "Well-tempered Clavier"). But the result was failure; the laborious work was wasted. Klengel had mistaken the means for the end; he had worked as a mathematician, not as a musician. Beethoven felt the true secret of Bach's greatness, and his own genius taught him how to profit by it. Next to the necessity of having something of importance to say, something which development will enhance, the great lesson which Beethoven learnt from Bach was unity in variety, the "highest law in all artistic creation," as Dr. H. Riemann well remarks in his *Catechism of Musical Æsthetics*.

Very many, probably the greater number, of Beethoven's sonatas rest upon some poetic basis. Bombet, in his *Life of Haydn*, tells us how that composer sometimes "imagined a little romance, which might furnish him with musical sentiments and colours"; and the titles which he gave to many of his symphonies certainly support that statement. At other times the romance was already to hand, as in the case of the 32nd sonata, which was inspired by Haydn's dear friend, Frau von Genziger. Of the

poetic basis underlying some of Beethoven's
sonatas we have fair knowledge.   Schindler, in
the second edition of his *Biography of Beethoven*,
gives a few extracts from the Conversation Books
(Conversations Hefte), in which, on account of the
master's deafness, questions or answers were
written down by those holding conversation with
him.   Beethoven read, and, of course, replied *viva
voce*.   We have not, it is true, his words, yet it is
possible, at times, to gather their purport from the
context.   For instance, there is a conversation (or
rather one half of it) recorded, which took place
in 1823 between the composer and Schindler.
The latter says : " Do you remember how I
ventured a few years ago to play over to you the
Sonata Op. 14 ?—now everything is clear."   The
next entry runs thus :—" I still feel the pain in
my hand."   A footnote explains that after
Schindler had played the opening section of the
first movement, Beethoven struck him somewhat
roughly on the hand, pushed him from the stool,
and, placing himself on it, played and *explained*
the sonata.   Then Schindler says : " Two prin-
ciples also in the middle section of ' Pathétique,' "
as if the teacher had called upon him to give
illustrations from other sonatas of what he had
explained concerning Op. 14.   But there is
another record of a conversation which took place
between Beethoven and Schindler in the very
month (March, 1827) in which the composer died.
" As you feel well to-day," says the disciple, " we

can continue our talk concerning the poetic basis ("wieder etwas poetisiren") of the Trio in B flat." And after some remarks about Aristotle's views of tragedy, and about the *Medea* of Euripides, we come across the following :—" But why *everywhere* a superscription ? In many movements of the sonatas and symphonies, where feeling and one's own imagination might dictate, such a heading would do harm. Music ought not, and cannot, on all occasions give a definite direction to feeling." Beethoven must have been alluding to some scheme of his for indicating the nature of the contents of his works, and its boldness seems to have astonished Schindler. It is possible that Beethoven, conscious that his end was not far distant, carried away by the enthusiasm of the moment, and desirous of giving all possible help to the right understanding of his music, went far beyond the modest lines by which he was guided when writing his "Pastoral" Symphony.[1] But let us return to the conversation.

" Good ! " says Schindler, " then you will next

[1] Schindler, by the way, relates in his *Biography of Beethoven* (3rd ed. 2nd Part, p. 212) that, already in 1816, when there was a proposal made by Hoffmeister to Beethoven to issue a new edition of his pianoforte music, the master conceived the intention of indicating the poetic idea (" Poetische Idee ") underlying his various works. And the biographer adds : " This term (*i.e. poetic idea*) belongs to Beethoven's epoch, and was used by him as frequently as was, for example, the expression ' poetic contents ' by others—in opposition to works which only often an harmonic and rhythmic play of tones. Writers on æsthetics of our day declaim against the latter term ; *with* good reason, if it refer to programme-music ; *without* reason,

set about writing an *angry* sonata?" Beethoven
would seem to have declared even that possible, for
Schindler continues: "Oh! I have no doubt you
will accomplish that, and I rejoice in anticipation."
And, then, as if remembering that his master was
an invalid, and that it would not be right to excite
him by prolonging the argument, he added, probably in a half-jocular manner: "Your housekeeper
must do her part, and first put you into a towering
passion." The above extracts show pretty clearly
that the poetic basis of his music was a subject
which Beethoven took pleasure in discussing with
his friends. Beethoven's back was, however, at
once up if he found others pushing the matter too
far. Of this we will give an instance. In the
year 1782 Dr. Christian Müller of Bremen organ-
ised concerts among the members of his family,
and, already at the beginning of the nineteenth
century, Beethoven's name figured on the programmes. A friend of the family, Dr. Carl Iken,
who took part in the musical proceedings, was an
ardent admirer of Beethoven's music, and he ventured to draw up explanations and picture-pro-
grammes of the master's works; and these were

if they extend their negation to all Beethoven's music, and deny its
poetic contents. Whence that tendency, which so frequently mani-
fests itself, and that strong desire to give pictorial explanations,
especially of the Beethoven symphonies and sonatas, if they contained nothing but a well-ordered harmonic and rhythmic play of
tones, and if they—or, at least, some of them—were not based on
some special idea? What other composer creates this almost
irresistible desire?"

read out before the performances of the works in question. It seems, indeed, that he was the first who felt impelled to give utterance to the poetical feelings aroused by Beethoven's music. Dr. Iken's intentions were of the best, and he may often have succeeded in throwing his audience into the right mood. A poetical programme, if not too fantastic, would often prove of better effect than the most skilful of analyses. These " Iken " programmes so delighted Dr. Müller that he sent several of them to the master at Vienna. Beethoven read, but his anger was stirred. He sent for Schindler, and dictated a letter to Dr. Müller. It was a friendly but energetic protest against such treatment of his or anyone else's music. He drew attention to the erroneous opinions to which it would give birth. *If explanations were needed*, he declared, *let them be limited to the general characteristics of the compositions*,[1] which it would not be difficult for cultured musicians to furnish. Thus relates Schindler, and there seems no reason to doubt his word. It is to be hoped that Dr. Müller's letter will one day be discovered. It was not the plan to which Beethoven objected, but the manner in which it was carried out.

[1] Mr. E. Pauer, in his preface to Ernst von Elterlein's *Beethoven's Pianoforte Sonatas explained for the lovers of the musical art*,— a valuable and interesting book,—remarks : " Herr von Elterlein's design is not so much to describe the beauties of Beethoven's sonatas, as to direct the performer's attention to these beauties, and to point out the *leading and characteristic features of each separate piece* " (the italics are ours).

Before quitting this subject, let us refer to one or two sonatas concerning which there are well authenticated utterances of the master. Schindler once asked him for the key to the Sonatas in D minor (Op. 31, No. 2) and F minor (" Appassionata "), and Beethoven replied : " Read Shakespeare's *Tempest*." The reply was laconic. Beethoven, no doubt, could have furnished further details, but he abstained from so doing, and in this he was perfectly justified. Then Schindler, growing bold, ventured a further question : "What did the master intend to express by the Largo of the Sonata in D (Op. 10, No. 3)?" And the latter replied that everyone felt that this Largo described the condition of the soul of a melancholy man, with various nuances of light and shade. Beethoven's quiet, dignified utterances deserve special attention in these days of programme-music. It is perhaps well that he did not carry out his idea of furnishing the clue to the poetic idea underlying his sonatas. It would, of course, have been highly interesting to know the sources of his inspirations, but it is terrible to think of the consequences which would have ensued. Composers would have imitated him, and those lacking genius would have made themselves and their art ridiculous. Berlioz went to extremes, but his genius saved him; and Schumann, a true poet, though inclined to superscriptions, kept within very reasonable lines.

It was undoubtedly this poetic basis that so affected the form of Beethoven's sonatas. The little

romances by which Haydn spurred his imagination were as children's tales compared with the
deep thoughts, the tragic events, and the masterpieces of Plato, Shakespeare, and Goethe, which
in Beethoven sharpened feeling and intensified
thought. The great sonatas of Beethoven are
not mere cunningly - devised pieces, not mere
mood-painting ; they are real, living dramas.

In aiming at a higher organisation, he actually
became a disorganiser. " All things are growing
or decaying," says Herbert Spencer. And in
Beethoven, so far as sonata and sonata-form are
concerned, we seem, as it were, to perceive the
beginning of a period of decay.

CHAPTER VIII

TWO CONTEMPORARIES OF BEETHOVEN

I. Weber

THE two greatest contemporaries of Beethoven
were, undoubtedly, Carl Maria von Weber and
Franz Schubert, and both wrote pianoforte sonatas.
Many other composers of that period—some of
them possessed of considerable talent—devoted
themselves to that branch of musical literature:
Steibelt (1764–1823), Woelfl (1772–1812), J. B.
Cramer (1771–1858), J. N. Hummel (1778–
1837), F. W. M. Kalkbrenner (1788–1849), and
others.   Of these, the first three may be named
sonata-makers.   The number which they produced is positively alarming; but it is some
consolation to think that a knowledge of their
works is not of essential importance.   Steibelt's
sonata in E flat (dedicated to Mme. Buonaparte)
was given once at the Popular Concerts in 1860,
and Woelfl's " Ne plus Ultra " sonata, several times
between 1859 and 1873; not one, however, of
the 105 said to have been written by J. B.

Cramer has ever been heard there.[1] Most of these works justly merit the oblivion into which they have fallen; some are quite second, or even third rate; others were written merely as show pieces,[2] and are now, of course, utterly out of date; and many were written for educational purposes, or to suit popular taste (sonatas containing variations on national and favourite airs, light rondos, etc.).[3]

Cramer's studies have achieved world-wide reputation, and, as music, they are often interesting. Also in his sonatas are to be found many serious,

[1] The Finale of a Sonata in A flat by Cramer, one of three dedicated to Haydn, is said to have suggested to Beethoven the Finale of *his* Sonata in A flat (Op. 26). Dr. Erich Prieger, who has recently published a facsimile of the autograph of Beethoven's sonata, in his preface quotes some passages from the Cramer Finale, which certainly seem to show that the Bonn master was to some extent influenced by his predecessor. Here is the second of the three passages quoted :—

[2] Woelfl's "Ne plus Ultra" Sonata would have long been forgotten but for Dussek's "Plus Ultra." See chapter on "Predecessors of Beethoven."

[3] In Steibelt's two sonatas (Op. 62), for instance, the airs "If a body meet a body," "Jesse Macpharlane," and "La Chrantreuse" are introduced. In his Op. 40 we also find "The Caledonian Beauty," "The Maid of Selma," "'Twas within a mile of Edinbro' town," and "Life let us cherish." Woelfl's sonatas (Op. 35, 38) also contain Scotch airs, and his "Ne plus Ultra" has variations on "Life let us cherish."

well-written movements; musical taste has, however, so changed since the rise of the romantic
school, that it is doubtful whether they would be
now acceptable even as teaching pieces.

Hummel's few sonatas have suffered at the
hand of time ; but, though the music be mechanical,
and therefore cold, there is much to interest
pianists in the two sonatas in F sharp minor
(Op. 81) and D major (Op. 106).   These were
written after the composer's appointment at Weimar
in 1820.   His two early sonatas (Op. 13, in E
flat, and Op. 20, dedicated to Haydn) are not easy,
yet not so difficult as the two just mentioned.

Steibelt and Woelfl both measured themselves
with Beethoven in the art of improvisation.   The
former was so ignominiously defeated that he
never ventured to meet his rival again.   Woelfl,
however, fared better.   With his long fingers he
could accomplish wonders on the instrument;
but only so far as technique was concerned did
he surpass Beethoven.

Carl Maria v. Weber (1786–1826) in early
youth studied the pianoforte under two able court
organists, J. P. Heuschkel[1] and J. N. Kalcher,[2]
both of whom he always held in grateful remembrance.   Under the direction of the latter he
wrote some pianoforte sonatas, which, according
to the statement of his son and biographer, M. M.
v. Weber, were accidentally destroyed.   Later on

[1] 1773–1853, court organist at Heldburghausen.
[2] 1766–1826, court organist at Freising.

he studied under Vogler and other masters. He became a famous pianist, and at Berlin, in 1812, composed his 1st Sonata in C (Op. 24). No. 2, in A flat (Op. 39), was commenced at Prague in 1814, and completed at Berlin in 1816. No. 3, in D minor (Op. 49), was also written at Berlin, and in the same year. No. 4, in E minor (Op. 70), occupied the composer between the years 1819 and 1822; it was written at Hosterwitz, near Dresden, during the time he was at work on his opera *Euryanthe*.

Weber and Schubert are both classed as contemporaries of Beethoven, yet the latter was also their predecessor. Of Schubert we shall speak presently. As regards Weber, it should be remembered that before he had written his sonata in C (Op. 24) Beethoven had already published "Les Adieux" (Op. 81A). The individuality of the composer of *Die Freischütz* was, however, so strong, that we meet with no direct traces of the influence of Beethoven in his pianoforte music.

The Weber sonatas have been described by Dr. P. Spitta as "fantasias in sonata-form," and this admirably expresses the character of these works. Weber followed the custom of his day in writing sonatas, but it seeems as though he would have accomplished still greater things had he given full rein to his imagination, and allowed subject-matter to determine form. Like his great contemporary, of whom we have next to speak, Weber, in spite

of Vogler's teaching, was not a strong contrapuntist; he relied chiefly upon melody, harmonic
effects, and strong contrasts. His romantic themes,
his picturesque colouring, enchant the ear, and
the poetry and passion of his pianoforte music,
both intensified by grand technique, stir one's soul
to its very depths; yet the works are of the
fantasia, rather than of the sonata order. We have
the letter rather than the true spirit of a sonata.
Place side by side Weber's Sonata in A flat (the
greatest of the four) and Beethoven's D minor or
" Appassionata," and the difference will be at once
felt. In the latter there is a latent power which is
wanting in the former. It seems as if one could
never sound the depths of Beethoven's music:
fresh study reveals new beauties, new details; the
relation of the parts to the whole (not only of the
sections of a movement, but of the movements *inter
se*), and, therefore, the unity of the whole becomes
more evident. We must not be understood to
mean that Weber worked without plan, or even
careful thought; but merely, that the organic
structure of his sonatas is far less closely knit
than in those of the Bonn master; there is contrast rather than concatenation of ideas, outward
show rather than inner substance. The slow
movements (with exception of those of the 1st
and 2nd Sonatas, which have somewhat of a
dramatic character) and Finales are satisfactory,
per se, as music: the former have charm, refinement; the latter, elegance, piquancy, brilliancy.

Now, in these sonatas, the opening movements seem like the commencement of some tragedy : in No. 2 there is nobility mixed with pathos ; in No. 3, fierce passion ; and in No. 4, still passion, albeit of a tenderer, more melancholy kind. But in the Finales it is as though we had passed from the tragedy of the stage to the melodrama, or frivolity of the drawing-room ; they offer, it is true, strong contrast, yet not of the right sort, not that to which Beethoven has accustomed us.

Throughout the four sonatas we detect the hand of a great pianist. In the first, the element of virtuosity predominates ; the first and, especially, the last movement (the so-called Perpetuum mobile) are show pieces, though of a high order. In the other sonatas the same element exists, and yet it seldom obtrudes itself ; the composer is merely using, to the full, the rich means at his command to express his luxuriant and poetical thoughts. In his writing for the instrument Weber recalls Dussek,—the Dussek of the " Retour à Paris " and " Invocation " sonatas. The earlier master was also a great pianist, and filled with the spirit of romance ; still he lacked the force and fire of Weber. Then, again, Dussek, in early manhood, passed through the classical crucible, whereas Weber was born and bred very much *à la Bohémienne* ; he developed from within rather than from without. It is easier to criticise than to create. If we cannot place the sonatas of Weber on the same high level as those of Beethoven, we may at least say that they take very high rank ; also, that in the hands of a great pianist they are certain to produce a powerful impression.

II. Schubert

The other great contemporary of Beethoven was Franz Schubert, born in 1797, the year in which the former published his Sonata in E flat (Op. 7). Then, again, Schubert's earliest pianoforte sonata was composed in February 1815, while Beethoven's Sonata in A (Op. 101) was produced at a concert only one year later (16th February 1816). It is well to remember these dates, by which we perceive that Beethoven had written twenty-seven of his thirty-two sonatas before Schubert commenced composing works of this kind. But though here and there the influence of the Bonn master may be felt in Schubert, the individuality of the latter was so strong, that we regard him as an independent contemporary. The influence of Haydn and Mozart, *plus* his own mighty genius, seem almost sufficient to account for Schubert's music. The new edition of the composer's works published by Messrs. Breitkopf & Härtel contains fifteen sonatas for pianoforte solo. The first four—

> No. 1, in E (1815),
> No. 2, in C (1815),
> No. 3, in A flat (1817), and
> No. 4, in E minor (1817),

had hitherto only been known by name.

In following the career of a great composer, his first efforts, however humble, however incomplete, are of interest; but from a purely musical point of view the Minuets of Nos. 2 and 3 are the most attractive portions of these sonatas; we catch in them glimpses of that freshness and romantic beauty which characterise Schubert's later productions.

In moments of strong inspiration, Schubert worked wonders, yet the lack of regular and severe study often makes itself felt. Though colouring may enhance counterpoint, it will not serve as a substitute for it. Then there is, at times, monotony of rhythm; and this, to a great extent, was the result of little practice in the art " of combining melodies."

While on the subject of Schubert's failings, we may as well complete the catalogue. In the later sonatas we meet with diffuseness; and sometimes a stroke of genius is followed by music which, at any rate for Schubert, is commonplace. It seems presumption to weigh the composer in critical balances, and to find him wanting; but he stands here side by side with Beethoven, and the contrast between the two men forces itself on our notice. Both were richly endowed by nature. By training, and the power of self-criticism which the latter brings with it, Beethoven was able to make the most of his gifts; Schubert, on the other hand, by the very lavish display which he sometimes made, actually weakened them. There is no page of musical history more touching than

the one which records how the composer, after
having written wonderful songs, grand symphonies,
and other works too numerous to mention, made
arrangements to study with S. Sechter, one of the
most eminent theorists of the day.   The composer
paid the latter a visit on the 4th November 1828;
but within a fortnight, Schubert was no longer in
the land of the living.   When too late, he seems to
have made the discovery which, perhaps, his very
wealth of inspiration had hidden from him up to
that moment, namely, that discipline strengthens
genius.   One may point out faults in Schubert's
art-works, yet his melodies and harmonies are so
bewitching, his music altogether so full of spontaneity and inspiration, that for the time being one
is spellbound.   Schumann was fairly right when
he described Schubert's lengths as " heavenly."

Three more sonatas were produced in the year
1817, the first in the unusual key of B major; and
here we find a marked advance in conception and
execution.   It opens with an Allegro, the total
effect of which, however, is not satisfactory; the
principal theme has dramatic power, and what
follows has lyrical charm, but the development
section is disappointing.   The Adagio seems like
an arrangement of a lovely symphonic movement;
the orchestra, and not the pianoforte, must have
been in the composer's mind when he penned it.
The lively Scherzo, with its quiet Trio, is a little
gem.   The clear-cut, concise form of such movements saved Schubert from all danger of diffuse-

ness ; and in them, as Mozart remarked to the
Emperor Joseph, who complained of the number
of notes in his opera, *Die Entführung*, there are
"just as many as are necessary." The sonata
in A minor (Op. 164), which consists of three
movements, is short and delightful from beginning
to end. In the opening Allegro the second
subject occurs, by way of exception, in the major
key of the submediant. There is much to admire
in the 3rd, in E flat, especially the Minuet and
Trio ; yet the music is not pure Schubert. About
six years elapsed between this and the next sonata,
in A minor (1823). Schubert had already written
his B minor Symphony, and though the first two
movements of the sonata will not compare with
those of the former in loftiness of conception,
there is a certain kinship between the two works.
In both there are fitful gusts of passion, a feeling
of awe, and a tone of sadness which tells of
disappointed hopes, of lost illusions. The Finale,
though fine, stands on a lower level. During the
years 1825–26, Schubert wrote, besides one in
A major (Op. 120), three magnificent sonatas : one
in A minor, dedicated to the Archduke Rudolph (Op.
42), another in D (Op. 53), and a third in G (Op. 78).
In these three works we have the composer's ripest
efforts. The first movement of the 1st, in A minor,
is well-nigh perfect. That opening phrase—

haunts one like a sad dream ; and the development

section, long, though not monotonous, is full of it. Without sacrificing his individuality, Schubert has here caught something of Beethoven's peculiar method of treating a theme,—that is, of evolving new phrases from its various sections. The coda, again, has penetrating power, and the fierce concluding phrase sounds like the passionate resistance of a proud artist to the stern degrees of fate. The tender melody and delicate variations of the Andante, the bold Scherzo, with its soft Trio, and the energetic Finale are all exceedingly interesting; yet they do not affect us like the first movement, in which lies not only the majesty, but the mystery of genius. The sonata in D has a vigorous opening Allegro,—a long, lovely, slow movement,—a crisp Scherzo, but a peculiar Finale, one which Schumann qualifies as comical (possirlich). The sonata in G contains some of the composer's most charming, characteristic music. The opening *moderato e cantabile* is a tone-poem of touching pathos. The sad principal theme is supported by such soft, tender harmonies, that its very sadness charms. In the development section it assumes a different character. Melancholy gives place to passion, at times fierce; then calm returns. The coda is one of the most fascinating ever penned by Schubert. The slow movement and Menuetto form worthy companions; but with the Finale the composer breaks the spell. Schumann says: " Keep away from it; it has no imagination, no enigma to solve."

The last three sonatas (in C minor, A, and B flat) were composed in September 1828, not three months before the death of the composer. In the opening theme of No. 2, determination and confidence are expressed, while in the Scherzo and Rondo there is even sunshine, though now and again black clouds flit across the scene. But in the Adagio, and in all the movements of the other two sonatas, the mood is either one of sadness, more or less intense, dark despair, or fierce frenzy. Music can express both joy and sorrow, though the latter seems more congenial to it. Mournful strains are an echo, as it were, of the " still, sad music of humanity." Grief, too, sharpens the imagination ; and music produced under its influence stirs a sensitive soul more powerfully than the brightest, merriest sounds. But these three sonatas, though they contain wonderful thoughts and some of Schubert's grandest, and most delicate harmonic colouring, fall short of perfection. They are too long, not because they cover so many pages, but because there is a lack of balance; at times, indeed, the composer seems to lose all sense of proportion. Then, again, the weakness of Schubert in the art of development is specially felt; the noble themes, on the whole, lose rather than gain by the loose, monotonous, and, in some places, even trivial treatment to which they are subjected. And what is more fatal than a lack of gradation of interest ? In a truly great work of art, be it poem, tragedy, sonata, or symphony, the

author carries his readers or audience along with
him from one point to another,—he gives no time
for rest or reflection; and when he has worked
them up to the highest pitch, he stops, and there
is an awakening, as it were, from some wonderful
dream. If afterwards the work be analysed, the
pains with which it was built up can be traced;
the powerful effect which it produced will be found
due, not alone to the creative power, the imagination of the author, but also to his dialectic skill and
to his critical faculty. It is all very well to talk of
great works as the fruits of hot inspiration and not
cold intellect. A masterpiece is the outcome of
both; the one provides the material, the other
shapes it. Schubert was an inspired composer, but
most of his works, especially those of large compass, show that he was mastered by moods, not
that he was master of them. It may be said that
many who can appreciate beautiful music have not
the bump of intellect strongly developed, and would
not therefore be affected by any such shortcomings;
that they would simply enjoy the music. That is
very likely, but here we are analysing and comparing; and neither the beauty nor even grandeur of
the music, nor the effect which it might produce
on certain minds, concerns us. There are many
persons who have had no technical training, but who
possess a true sense of order, proportion, and gradation; and such instinctively feel that Schubert's
sonatas, in spite of their many striking qualities,
are not so great as those of Beethoven. We have

referred more than once to the Popular Concert catalogue, which is a very fair thermometer of public taste. One can see how seldom the Schubert sonatas are performed in comparison with those of his great contemporary. But to refer specially to the three last sonatas now under notice. The one in B flat (No. 3) was played by Mr. Leonard Borwick, it is true, on the 3rd February 1894, but the previous date of performance was 16th January 1882. No. 2, in A, was last given in 1882, and No. 1 has not been heard since 1879.

The Allegro of the C minor sonata opens with a bold theme, and an energetic transition passage leads to the dominant of the relative major key. Of the soft second theme Schubert seems so fond, that he is loth to quit it; he repeats it in varied form, and still after that, it is heard in minor. This unnecessarily lengthens the exposition section, which, in addition, has the repeat mark. The development section is rather vague, but the coda is impressive: the long descending phrase and the sad repeated minor chords at the close suggest exhaustion after fierce conflict. The theme of the Adagio, in A flat, partly inspired by Beethoven, is noble, and full of tender, regretful feeling; the opening and close of the movement are the finest portions. The Minuet and Trio are effective, but the final Allegro is hopelessly long, and by no means equal to the rest of the work.

The first movement of the sonata in A has a characteristic principal theme, and one in the

dominant key of bewitching beauty. The coda
gives a last reminiscence of the opening theme ;
but its almost defiant character has vanished
away; for it is now played pianissimo. Schubert,
in the importance of his codas, recalls Beethoven ;
each, however, made it serve a different purpose.
The latter, at any rate in his Allegro movements,
gathers together his strength, as if for one last,
supreme effort. Schubert, on the other hand,
seems rather as if his strength were spent, and
as if he could only give a faint echo of his leading
theme. The coda of the first movement of the
sonata in A minor (Op. 42) offers, however, one
striking exception. The Andantino and Scherzo
of the A sonata are well-nigh perfect, but the
Rondo, in spite of much that is charming, is of
inferior quality and of irritating length. The 3rd
sonata, in B flat, the last of the series, the *sonate-
testament*, as Von Lenz said of Beethoven's
Op. 111, has wonderful moments, yet it contains also lengths which even Schumann would
scarcely have ventured to style " heavenly." We
refer particularly to the first and last movements ;
the Andante and Scherzo are beyond criticism.

These sonatas were written as Schubert was
about to enter the Valley of the Shadow of Death.
His spirit was still strong, but his flesh must have
been weak. To turn away from them on account
of any imperfections, would be to lose some of
Schubert's loftiest thoughts, some of his choicest
tone-painting.

CHAPTER IX

AFTER Beethoven, the first composer of note was Robert Schumann, one of the founders of the so-called romantic school. In one of his letters he refers to Beethoven's choral symphony " as the turning-point from the classical to the romantic period." By reading, Schumann had cultivated his imagination, but his musical training was irregular; and, indeed, when he first commenced composing, practically *nil*. If his soul was stirred by some poem, or tale, or by remembrance of some dear friend, he sought to express his thoughts and feelings, and on the spur of the moment. In a letter he writes : " I have been all the week at the piano, composing, writing, laughing, and crying, all at once. You will find this state of things nicely described in my Op. 20, the ' Grosse Humoreske,' which is already at the printer's. You see how quickly I always work now. I get an idea, write it down, and have it printed ; that's what I like. Twelve sheets composed in a week ! " And thus short-tone poems, or a long piece, such as the " Humoreske," of irregular form, were the result. Now that was not the way in which he composed his two sonatas. He was two years, off and on, at work on the first, in F sharp minor (Op. 11), and eight on the other, in G minor (Op. 22). One may therefore conclude that the fetters of form were a source of trouble to him. And he can scarcely have felt very enthusiastic over his task; in 1839, after both sonatas were completed, he declared that " although from time to time fine specimens of the sonata species made their appearance, and, probably, would continue to do so, it seemed as if that form of composition had run its appointed course."

Of the two sonatas, the one in F sharp minor is the more interesting. The Aria is a movement of exquisite simplicity and tenderness, and the Scherzo, with its *Intermezzo alla burla*, has life and character. But the Allegro, which follows the poetical introduction, and the Finale are patchy, and at times laboured. It must not, however, be supposed that they are uninteresting. The music has poetry and passion, and the strong passages atone for the weak ones. There were composers at that time who could produce sonatas more correct in form, and more logical in treatment, yet not one who could have written music so filled with the spirit of romance.

The Sonata in G minor resembles its predecessor both in its strong and its weak points. Considered, however, as a whole, it is less warm, less intense.

It is unnecessary to describe the two works in detail, for they must be familiar to all musicians, and especially pianists.   A sympathetic rendering of them will always give pleasure; but in a history of evolution they are of comparatively small moment. It is interesting to compare them with the Fantasia in C (Op. 17), a work in which Schumann displayed the full power of his genius.

Chopin was another composer whose spirit moved uneasily within the limits of the sonata. The first which he wrote (we do not reckon the posthumous one in C minor)—the one in B flat minor—is an impressive work.   There is a certain rugged power in the opening movement, and the Scherzo is passionate, and its Trio tender.   The picturesque March owes much of its effect to its colouring and contrasts; while the extraordinary Finale sounds weird and uncanny.   In the hands of a great interpreter the music makes a powerful appeal; yet as a sonata it is not really great. It lacks organic development, unity.   The Sonata in B minor, though attractive to pianists, is an inferior work.   The first movement, with exception of its melodious second theme, is dry, and the Finale belongs to the *bravoura* order of piece.   The Scherzo is light and graceful.   The slow movement is the most poetical of the four, though spun out at too great length.   The real Chopin is to be found in his nocturnes, mazurkas, and ballads, not in his sonatas.

Among modern sonatas, the three by Brahms

(C, Op. 1 ; F sharp minor, Op. 2 ; and F minor, Op. 5) claim special notice. With the exception of the Liszt Sonata in B minor, which, whatever its musical value, at least opens up " new paths " in the matter of form, the Brahms sonatas are the only ones since Schumann which distinctly demand detailed notice. The composer followed ordinary Beethoven lines ; with exception of the Intermezzo of the 3rd Sonata, the number and order of movement resemble those of many a Beethoven sonata ; while there is enlargement, not change in the matter of form. Brahms studied the special means by which his great predecessor, in some instances, sought to accentuate the unity between various sections of a sonata ; he steeped his soul in the romantic music of Beethoven, Schubert, Chopin, and Schumann, and, in addition, trained his intellect to grasp the mysteries of counterpoint, and to perceive the freer modern uses to which it was put by the classical masters. Brahms' early acquaintance with Liszt opened up to him, too, the resources of modern technique. And thus, possessing individuality of his own, in addition to these inheritances and acquirements, Brahms wrote sonatas, which, though in the main on old lines, are no mere imitations, pale reflexes of his predecessors.

The 1st Sonata, in C (Op. 1), has for its opening theme one which has been said to resemble the opening theme of Beethoven's Op. 106. It will be well to look on this picture (Beethoven)—

and on this (Brahms)—

There is resemblance in the matter of rhythm, but the up-beat in Beethoven constitutes a marked difference; and, besides, the succession of notes differs in each case. Brahms's theme, already at the eighth bar, recommences in a key a tone lower; a similar proceeding, by the way, is to be found in Beethoven's Sonata in G (Op. 31, No 1). After a few points of imitation, and digression through various keys, we meet with a new theme in A minor, the soft, tender character of which contrasts well with the bold opening one. But unity amid diversity is Brahms' aim; and here the contrast does not prevent a certain kinship between them—one, however, which can be felt rather than explained.[1] Of another pianissimo phrase, still in A minor, much use is afterwards made. The prominence given in the exposition section to the subject-matter styled "secondary," and still more so in the development section, is peculiar; this feature had certainly not been copied from Beethoven, who, as a rule, made his first

[1] Notice, in each case, the falling interval in the second and fourth bar.

theme of first importance. Brahms concludes his exposition section in the opening key of the movement,—a return to early methods ; Beethoven adopted a similar course in the first movement of his Op. 53. Brahms' development section is comparatively short. Of counterpoint we get a good illustration in the combinations of both first and second themes ; of colour, in the presentation of the mournful minor theme in the major key ; and of originality, in the bars leading to the recapitulation. In this last instance, the idea of gradually drawing closer together the members of a phrase was borrowed from Beethoven, but not the manner in which it is carried out. In the earlier master it often stands out as a special feature ; here we have, besides, counter rhythm, and ambiguous modulation. When the principal theme returns, it is clothed first with sub-dominant, then with tonic minor harmony. The movement concludes with a vigorous coda evolved from the opening theme. Five bars from the end, the first two bars of that theme are given out in their original form ; and then, as if repetition were not sufficient, a thematic cadence is added, in which the notes are given in loud tones, in augmented form, and, in addition, with slackened *tempo* (*largamente*). The slow movement (Andante) was, we believe, one of Brahms' earliest efforts at composition ; it is said to have been written by him at the age of fourteen. It consists of a theme with variations ; and the former is based on an old

German Minnelied.   The words of the folk song
are written beneath the notes, as if to put the
listener into the right mood.[1]   We need not dwell
on the variations, in which Beethoven and
Schubert are the prevailing influences, though
not to any alarming extent.   The music is by no
means difficult; for Brahms, indeed, remarkably
easy.   The movement opens in C minor, but
closes in C major.   A Scherzo follows (E minor,
six-eight time; Allegro molto e con fuoco); it
has a trio in C major.   The Scherzo, with its
varied rhythm, is full of life ; the Trio, interesting
in harmony, and also in the matter of rhythm.
The Finale (another Allegro con fuoco; the
young composer has mounted his fiery Pegasus)
opens in C, in nine-eight time, thus—

 etc.

a metamorphosis, in fact, of the opening theme of
the sonata.   And later on we have a similar
re-presentation of subject-matter from the first
movement.   This Finale is musically and
technically attractive, yet scarcely on the same
high level as the first movement.   But the age of
the composer must be taken into consideration ;
for quite a young man, it is a wonderful
production.

The 2nd Sonata (Op. 2) is in F sharp minor.
The Allegro non troppo ma energico is a move-

[1] Verstohlen geht der Mond auf, blau, blau Blümelein, etc.

ment which in its subject-material breathes the
spirit of Chopin : the weird, stormy opening in the
principal key may claim kinship with the opening
of the Polish composer's " Polonaise " in the same
key ; while a certain strain in the melodious
second subject brings to one's mind a Chopin
Nocturne, also in F sharp minor ; in neither case,
however, is there anything amounting to plagiarism.
The exposition section is not repeated. The
development is clever, though, perhaps, somewhat
formal. Again here, the secondary theme occupies,
apparently, chief attention ; but it is supported by
a bass evolved from a principal motive. And in
transition passages of the exposition, and also in
the recapitulation section and coda—

in one or other shape, makes itself heard ; so that,
though outwardly subordinate, its function is
important : it binds together various portions of
the movement, and thus promotes union. The
Andante which follows, consists, as in the 1st
Sonata, of a theme with variations. There is
nothing novel either in the theme or its mode of
treatment. Certain chords, cadences, figures,
suggest Schubert—an idol whom Brahms has
never ceased to worship ; and, in one place, the
three staves, and a few passages, show the
influence of Liszt, the pianist *par excellence* of the
days in which this sonata was written ; but the

movement has, in addition to romantic charm,
individuality. It commences in B minor; then
after a short expressive passage in major, an
arpeggio chord leads directly to the Scherzo; the
following shows the outward connection between
the two movements—

This bright, clever Scherzo, with its soft
Schubertian trio, need not detain us. The final
Allegro is preceded by a short introduction, in
which the chief theme and other material of the
Finale are set forth. The connection between this
and the earlier movements of the sonata is not
evident, like the one, for instance, already noticed,
between the Andante and the Scherzo; with
research, and possibly some imagination, relationship might, however, be traced. We are far
from asserting that movements of a sonata ought
to be visibly connected; after all, the true bond of
union must be a spiritual one. But if an attempt
be made in that direction, surely the opening and
closing movements are those which, by preference,
should be selected. In his Op. 28 Beethoven seems
to have evolved the themes of all four movements
from the first; in Op. 106 and Op. 109, connection is clear between the first and last movements. Such an experiment was safe in the
hands of Beethoven, and Brahms has never

allowed it to become a mannerism; but second-rate composers, and superficial listeners run the danger of mistaking the shadow for the substance. To this matter we shall, however, soon return. Many references have been made to the composers who have influenced Brahms, yet we cannot resist naming one more. The opening section of this Allegro Finale reminds one more than once of the corresponding section in Clementi's fine Sonata in B minor. The music of this concluding movement is clever.

The 3rd sonata (Op. 5) is in F minor. The Allegro opens with a wild, sinister theme, and one which even casts a shadow over the calm, hope-inspiring strains afterwards heard in the orthodox key of the relative major. The tender melodies and soft chromatic colouring which fill the remainder of the exposition section show strong feeling for contrast. Again, storm and stress alternate with comparative calm in the development section. The Andante expressivo bears the following super-scription :—

> Der Abend dämmert, das Mondlicht scheint
> Da sind zwei Herzen in Liebe vereint
> Und halten sich selig umfangen.
>
> *—Sternau.*

And it offers a delightful tone-picture. The moon " o'er heaven's clear azure spreading her sacred light," the calm of evening, and happy, though ever-sighing, lovers : 'tis a scene to tempt poet, painter, and musician. The last, however, seems to have greatest advantage; music by imitation and association can describe scenes of nature; and it can paint, for are not its harmonies colours? But the musician can do what is possible to neither poet nor painter,—he can make a direct appeal to the emotions in their own language. The soft, dreamy coda—which, with its Andante molto, its Adagio, and widened-out closing cadence, seems to indicate the unwillingness of the lovers to part—has Schubert colouring and charm. The reminiscence, at the commencement of this movement, of the middle movement of the "Pathétique" cannot fail to attract attention. Then, again, the opening of the Scherzo [1] —

sounds familiar. It must surely have been this movement in which someone pointed out to the composer a reminiscence of Mendelssohn. "Anyone can find that out," was the rough-and-ready reply of Brahms. But if Mendelssohn be the prevailing influence in the Scherzo, Schubert has his turn in the Trio. The fourth movement is an Intermezzo, entitled "Rückblick" (Retrospect). The opening phrase, and indeed the whole of the short movement, carries us back to the picture of the lovers. Some change has taken place: have the lovers grown cold? or has death divided them? The

[1] The long arpeggio leading up to the first note is omitted.

themes are now sad, and clothed in minor harmonies. The Finale, perhaps, shows skill rather than inspiration; with regard to some of the subject-matter, it is, like the previous movement, also retrospective.

Liszt's sonata in B minor, dedicated to Robert Schumann, was evidently written under the special influence of Beethoven's later sonatas,—perhaps more particularly the one in A flat, Op. 110. There is by no means unanimity of opinion among musicians with regard to Liszt's merit as a composer; some consider that his genius has not yet been properly recognised; others, that he will not for a moment bear comparison with any one of the great masters who preceded him, and who wrote for the pianoforte. Among his works which have specially given rise to discussion stands this B minor Sonata, which has proved a stumbling-block, both on account of its form and its contents. It would simplify matters if the one could be discussed without the other; this, however, is not possible.

We have hitherto considered the sonata of three movements as typical, and from that type Liszt's work differs; yet not " so widely, as on a first hearing or reading may appear." Thus wrote Mr. C. A. Barry in a remarkably interesting analysis of the sonata which he prepared some years back for Mr. Oscar Beringer. He remarks further: " All the leading characteristics of a sonata in three movements are here fully maintained within the scope of a single movement, or, to speak more precisely,

an uninterrupted succession of several changes of
tempo, thus constituting a more complete organism
than can be attained by three distinct and independent movements."

The idea of passing from one movement to
another without break dates from Emanuel Bach,
nay, earlier, from Kuhnau; and Beethoven occasionally adopted it, and with striking effect. The
wretched habit at concerts of applauding between
the movements of a sonata establishes a break
where—at any rate in certain sonatas of Beethoven
—the composer certainly imagined an *uninterrupted*
succession. The second movement of the "Appassionata" breaks off with an arpeggio chord of
diminished seventh, and the Finale starts on the
same chord. Yet surely after the final tonic chord
of the opening Allegro there should be no break,
but only a brief pause. A *fermata* in the middle
of a movement does not constitute a break, neither
need it at the end. In Beethoven's sonatas we
find many movements, outwardly independent,
yet inwardly connected; those of the D minor and
F minor may be named by way of illustration.
The composer, however, in one or two of his
works, revived, to some extent, the plan adopted
in the suites of early times, of evolving various
movements from one theme. Such outward connection may help to strengthen a bond of union
already existing, but it will not establish it. The
question, then, of Liszt's "more complete organism"
depends, after all, on the contents of the music.

So, too, when, in addition to uninterrupted succession, Liszt makes the one theme of the slow introduction the source whence he derives the principal part of his tone-picture, everything depends on the quality and latent power of this fertilising germ. Discussion of form *per se* is an impossibility. This Liszt sonata stands, however, as a bold attempt to modify a form which, as we have seen, Schumann thought exhausted (was it for that reason that Liszt dedicated the work to him ?), and one in which so many soulless compositions were written during the second quarter of the present century. " La sonate," says Charles Soullier in his *Nouveau Dictionnaire de Musique Illustré*, " est morte avec le dix-huitième siècle qui en a tant produit." Is Liszt's sonata a Phœnix rising from its ashes ? Shall we be able to say " La sonate est morte ! Vive la sonate ! " Time will tell. Hitherto Liszt's work has not borne fruit.

CHAPTER X

THE SONATA IN ENGLAND

IN previous chapters we have been occupied with Italy and Germany. Without reference to those countries a history of the pianoforte sonata would be impossible. Italy was the land of its birth; Germany, that of its growth, and, apparently, highest development. During the sixteenth and seventeenth centuries England furnished notable composers for the harpsichord. William Byrd and Dr. John Bull are not only among the earliest, but at the time in which they flourished, they were the greatest who wrote for a keyboard instrument. At the beginning of the seventeenth century English music was indeed in a prosperous state; it was admired at home, and its merits were acknowledged abroad. H. Peacham, in his *Compleat Gentleman*, published in the reign of James I., says of Byrd: "For motets and musicke of piety, devotion, as well as for the honour of our nation, as the merit of the man, I preferre above all others our Phœnix, Mr William Byrd, whom in that kind I know not whether any may equall. I am sure none excell, even by the judgement of France and Italy, who are very sparing in their commendation of strangers, in regard of that conceipt they hold of themselves. His ' Cantiones Sacrae,' as also his ' Gradualia,' are mere angelicall and divine ; and being of himselfe naturally disposed to gravity and piety his veine is not so much for light madrigals or canzonets ; yet his ' Virginella,' and some others in his first set, cannot be mended by the first Italian of them all." Then at the end of the seventeenth century came Purcell, a genius who seemed likely to raise English music still higher in the estimation of foreign musicians. But, alas ! he departed ere his powers were matured ; by his death English art sustained a grievous loss, and from that time declined. The history of instrumental music during the eighteenth century is dull, and, so far as the pianoforte sonata is concerned, of little or no importance. Nevertheless, a brief survey of that century will be attempted, after which reference will be made to a few sonata composers of the century now drawing to a close. Just as we referred to the sonatas for strings and harpsichord before commencing the history of the clavier-sonata proper, so here a few remarks will be made concerning the sonata before Dr. T. A. Arne—the first composer, so far as we can trace, who wrote a work of that kind for the harpsichord alone.

In 1683 appeared Purcell's Twelve Sonatas for two violins and a bass, the very same year in

which Corelli published *his* " Twelve Sonatas " (Op.
1).   In his preface, Purcell frankly admits that
" he has faithfully endeavoured a just imitation of
the most famed Italian masters."   Sir J. Hawkins
supposes that "the sonatas of Bassani,[1] and perhaps
of some other of the Italians, were the models
after which he formed them."   In our introductory
chapter we mentioned the sonatas (" a due, trè,
quattro, e cinque stromenti ") by Vitali (1677); and
of these, Mr. J. A. Fuller-Maitland, in his preface to
the Purcell Society edition of the "Twelve Sonatas"
of 1683, remarks that " it is difficult to resist the
conclusion that these were the Englishman's
models."   Vitali undoubtedly exerted strong influence; yet Purcell himself describes his " Book of
Sonatas " as " a just imitation of the most fam'd
Italian Masters."   These sonatas of 1683, also
the ten which appeared after his death (among

---

[1] In the British Museum copy the " XII. Sonate da Chiesa, Opera
Quinta " of Bassani are bound up with " Sonate a Tre " by Giacomo
Sherard.   In plain English, the latter composer was a certain James
Sherard, an apothecary by profession.   The Bassani sonatas here
mentioned were published at Amsterdam.   Hawkins tells us that
" an ordinary judge, not knowing that they were the work of another,
might mistake them for compositions of Corelli."   The first violin
book has the following entry :—" Mr. Sherard was an apothecary
in Crutched Friars about the year 1735, performed well on the violin,
was very intimate with Handel and other Masters."   This copy,
which possibly belonged to Sherard, contains also the following,
written apparently by the person into whose hands the book passed :
—" Wm. Salter, surgeon and apothecary, Whitechapel High
Street."   The various sonatas, too, are marked in pencil—some
as *good*; others, *very good*.   The date, 1789, is also given—the year,
probably, in which the volumes became the property of W. Salter.

which is to be found No. 9, called the " Golden
Sonata ") in 1697, are of great importance and
interest in the history of English music, but there
is no new departure in them ; this, at any rate in
the earlier ones of 1683, is fully acknowledged by
the composer.

In 1695, John Ravenscroft, a descendant,
possibly, of Thomas Ravenscroft, published at
Rome, sonatas for " violini, e violine, o arciliuto, col
basso per l'organo " Opera prima, but they were
mere imitations of Corelli.[1]   In 1728 a certain
John Humphries published by subscription " Twelve
Sonatas for two violins and a bass "; and Hawkins,
in his *History*, excites curiosity by declaring
that they are " of a very original cast " ; he adds,
however, " in respect that they are in a style somewhat above that of the common popular airs and
country dance tunes, the delight of the vulgar, and
greatly beneath what might be expected from the
studies of a person not at all acquainted with the
graces and elegancies of the Italians in their compositions for instruments.   To this it must be
attributed that the sonatas of Humphries were
the common practice of such small proficients in
harmony as in his time were used to recreate
themselves with music at alehouse clubs and places
of vulgar resort in the villages adjacent to London ;

---

[1] These sonatas were afterwards published at Amsterdam as
Corelli's, being marked as his Opera Settima.   On the title-page
was written "Si crede che Siano State Composte di Arcangelo
Corelli avanti le sue altre Opere."

of these there were formerly many, in which six-
pence, at most, was the price of admission." We
have quoted this passage at length, because it indirectly confirms our statement concerning English
music of this period. If Hawkins had had anything better to talk about, he would not have
wasted space on the music of alehouses and
" places of vulgar resort." It may, however, be
asked whether Hawkins' report of Humphries'
music is trustworthy. Now, although the sonatas
offer nothing of special interest, we may certainly
venture to say that one does not hear such well-
written melodious strains in or near alehouses of
the present day. The sonatas consist, for the most
part, of four short movements. First, a slow introduction, then an Allegro somewhat in the Corelli
style. An Adagio, often very short, separates this
from the final movement, an Allegro in binary form,
a Minuet, or a Gigue. This " Humphries" musical
landmark is the only one we have to offer our
readers between Purcell and Dr. Arne. But before
proceeding to notice the sonatas of the latter, let
us say something, if not of English music, yet of
music in England during the first half of the
eighteenth century.

Of the influence of Corelli we have already
made mention. That influence was materially
strengthened by the two celebrated violinist-
composers, Veracini and Geminiani, who came
to London in 1714; the former only paid a
short visit; the latter made England his home.

Then a greater composer than the two just mentioned had already arrived in London; this was Handel, whose Rinaldo had been produced with wonderful success on the 24th February 1710. The genius of Handel triumphed over all rivals, whether English or foreign, for well-nigh half a century; and this fact alone explains the decline of English art. But there was another strong influence which specially affected harpsichord music: the Lessons of Domenico Scarlatti had made their way throughout Europe. Thomas Roseingrave, who went to Italy in 1710, became acquainted with the composer, and on his return pleaded the cause of the Italian with an enthusiasm similar to that displayed a century later by Samuel Wesley for Scarlatti's great contemporary, J. S. Bach. Roseingrave edited " Forty-two Suites of Lessons for the Harpsichord " by Scarlatti. Still another Italian influence may be mentioned. "On the day," says Burney in his *History of Music*, " when Handel's Coronation Anthem was rehearsed at Westminster Abbey (1727) San Martini's [1] twelve sonatas were advertised." But Handel and Scarlatti make up the history of harpsichord music in England during the first half of the eighteenth century. Burney expressly states that " the Lessons of the one and the Suites of the other were the only good music for keyed instruments."

Thomas Augustine Arne (1710-78) is prin-

[1] See chapter on Haydn.

cipally known as a writer of operas and incidental
music to plays, but he also wrote organ concertos,
and sonatas for the harpsichord.   The latter,
entitled " VIII. Sonatas or Lessons for the
Harpsichord," probably appeared somewhere about
1750.   With this double title it is, of course,
impossible to regard them as serious sonatas.
No. 8, for instance, consists merely of a Minuet
with variations !   No. 1 opens with an Andante
in binary form, while two bars of Adagio lead to
another Allegro of similar structure.   No. 2 is of
a similar kind.   The binary form is of the later
type, *i.e.* there is a return to the principal theme
in the second section.   No. 3 opens with a Prelude, and a note states that " in this and other
Preludes, which are meant as extempore touches
before the Lesson begins, neither the composer nor
performer are oblig'd to a Strictness of Tune." The
pleasing Allegro which follows shows the influence
of Scarlatti-Handel.   The sonata concludes with
an attractive Minuet and variations.   No. 5, with
its graceful Gavotta, and No. 7 might be performed
occasionally.   Arne's sonatas, if not great, contain
some neat, melodious writing.

The second half of the century still offers poor
results so far as national music is concerned.   We
have spoken of Handel and Scarlatti ; but, after
them, music in England again fell under foreign rule.
In the very year of Handel's death, John Christian
Bach arrived in London, which he made his home
until his death in 1782.   During that period the

sonatas of Mozart and Haydn became known; and
the two visits of the latter to England in 1791–92
and 1794–95 gave greater lustre to his name, and
rendered his style still more popular. And all this
foreign influence (strong inasmuch as Haydn and
Mozart belonged to a school with which J. C.
Bach was in sympathy) is reflected in the English
music of the period. John Burton published, in
1766, "Ten Sonatas for the Harpsichord,"
which are of interest. Some of the writing
recalls Scarlatti, but there are also many
touches of harmony and melody which tell of later
times. The introduction of the Alberti bass is
one clear sign of a post-Scarlatti period. Burton
paid a visit to Germany in 1752, and was, we
presume, acquainted with Emanuel Bach's compositions. We may also name six sonatas by
I. Worgan, M.B., published in 1769. At the head
of No. 5, the composer remarks: "Lest the consecutive fifths at the beginning of the theme of this
movement should escape the critic, the author here
apprizes him of them." They are as follows:—

The critic of those days must have been very
dull if he required such assistance, and his ear
very sensitive if offended by such consecutives as
these. Lastly, we may give the name of a lady,

Miss Barthélémon,[1] whose interesting Sonata in G (Op. 3) was dedicated to Haydn.

In the early part of the nineteenth century, John Field, whose nocturnes are still played and admired, wrote three sonatas (Op. 1), and dedicated them to Muzio Clementi, his teacher.   No. 1 is in E flat; No. 2, in A; and No. 3, in C minor. They all consist of only two movements (No. 1, Allegro and Rondo; No. 2, Allegro and Allegro Vivace; No. 3, Allegro and Allegretto).   In the first two sonatas the two movements are in the same key; in the last, the first movement is in C minor, the second, in C major.   The Rondo of No. 1 contains foreshadowings of Chopin.   Field's music, generally, is old-fashioned, and not worth revival; none, indeed, of his sonatas have ever been played at the Monday Popular Concerts.

Samuel Wesley[2] wrote three sonatas (Op. 3), likewise eight, dedicated to the Hon. Daynes Barrington, yet we fear that not one of them would prove acceptable at the present day.   One looks in vain for the name of Wesley in the

[1] She was surely the daughter of François Hippolite Barthélémon (son of a Frenchman and of an Irish lady), who was on intimate terms with Haydn, to whom the sonata above mentioned is dedicated.

[2] Samuel Wesley (1766–1837), nephew of the Rev. John Wesley, was a gifted musician, and is specially remembered for his enthusiastic admiration of John Sebastian Bach.   The letters which he wrote to Benjamin Jacob on the subject of his favourite author were published by his daughter in 1875.   He also, in conjunction with C. F. Horn, published an edition of Bach's "Wohltemperirtes Clavier."

Popular Concert Catalogue.   Cipriani Potter
(1792–1871)   deserves   a   word   of   mention.
Beethoven, writing to Ries, in London, in 1818,
says: "Potter has visited me several times; he
seems to be a good man, and has talent for composition."   His Sonata in C (Op. 1, dedicated to
Mrs. Brymer Belcher) consists of three movements :
an Allegro non troppo with a Haydnish theme—

 etc.

an attractive Adagio, and a dainty and pleasing
Rondo pastorale.   The influence of Beethoven
and Clementi is great; the individuality of Potter,
small.   But the sonata is thoroughly well written,
and—at any rate as an educational piece—the
Rondo deserves reprinting.

Sir G. A. Macfarren composed three sonatas
for the pianoforte.   No. 3, in G minor, dedicated
to Miss Agnes Zimmermann, is a work which
presents several features of interest.   In the first
long movement (an Allegro moderato) there is no
repeat.   The exposition section really contains
three subjects: an opening one in the principal
key, a second in D flat, and a third in the orthodox
key of the relative major.   The development
section, in which there is some solid counterpoint,
is decidedly clever; much use is made in it of the
second subject mentioned above.   The Andante
is a movement of simple structure.   A brisk
Scherzo, in the making of which Weber and

Schumann seem to have lent a helping hand, leads to a long Finale,—the last, but by no means the most successful of the four movements. We have just spoken of influences; Weber may be said to have presided at the birth of the opening Allegro, and Mendelssohn at that of the Finale. The appearance in the Finale of the D flat theme from the Allegro deserves note. This sonata may not be an inspired work, yet it has many excellent qualities.

Of Sir Sterndale Bennett's two sonatas, the 1st, in F minor (Op. 13, dedicated to Mendelssohn), commences with a long movement (Moderato expressivo), in which there are traces of the master to whom it is dedicated; it is followed by a clever Scherzo and Trio, a melodious Serenata, and a weak Presto agitato. The first, second, and last movements are in F minor, the third in F major. Schumann, in a brief notice of the work, describes it as excellent. The sonata (Op. 46) entitled "The Maid of Orleans" commences with an Andante pastorale in A flat, above which are written the following lines from Act iv. Scene 1 of Schiller's play, *Die Jungfrau von Orleans*:—

> "Schuldlos trieb ich meine Lämmer
> Auf des stillen Berges Höh."

> "In innocence I led my sheep
> Adown the mountain's silent steep."

The movement is graceful and pleasing. Then follows an Allegro marziale:—

"Den Feldruf hör ich mächtig zu mir dringen
Das Schlactross steigt, und die Trompeten klingen."
                                    Prologue : Scene 4.

"The clanging trumpets sound, the chargers rear,
And the loud war cry thunders in mine ear."

Then an "In Prison" section with suitable superscription —

"Höre mich, Gott, in meiner höchsten Noth," etc.
                                    Act v. Scene 2.

"Hear me, O God, in mine extremity."

Lastly, a Finale —

"Kurz ist das Schmerz, und ewig ist die Freude."
                                    Act v. Scene 14.

"Brief is the sorrow, endless is the joy."

The title and the various superscriptions naturally cause the sonata to be ranked as programme-music, but of a very simple kind. It is easy to suggest pastoral scenes : a few pedal notes, a certain simplicity of melody, and a few realistic touches expressive of the waving of branches of trees, or the meandering of a brook, and the thing is accomplished.

Dr. C. H. Parry is an English composer whose name has of late been much before the public. He has written works both secular and sacred for our important provincial festivals ; also chamber music, songs, etc. ; and all his music shows mastery of form, skill in the art of development, and eclectic taste. For the present, we are,

however, concerned merely with his sonatas.   Like
Brahms, he at first composed pianoforte sonatas :
No. 1, in F; No. 2, in A minor and major.
Brahms made a third attempt, but the two just
mentioned are all that are known to us of Dr.
Parry's.   No. 1 opens with a non troppo Allegro,
a smooth movement of somewhat pastoral character ; the music, also the writing for the instrument,
remind one occasionally of Stephen Heller.   A
bright, though formal Scherzo, with a well-contrasted Trio in the key of the submediant, is
followed by a melodious Andante and a graceful,
showy Allegretto.

No. 2 has an introductory movement marked
maestoso ; it is divided into three sections.   The
first opens with a phrase of dramatic character ;
the second, in the remote key of G sharp minor,
contains two short, expressive, Schumannish
themes treated in imitation ; the third has
passages leading back to the opening key and
phrase.   The Allegro grazioso which follows is a
compact little movement ; in form it is orthodox,
yet there is no repeat to the exposition section.
The influence of Heller is still felt, but also that
of Schumann.   Grace rather than power distinguishes the Adagio con sentimento, in the key
of C sharp minor.   The Scherzo is clever and effective, and the Allegretto cantabile, though the last,
is scarcely the best of the four movements.

A manuscript Sonata in D flat (Op. 20) by Dr.
C. V. Stanford, another prominent composer of

our day, was produced at the Popular Concerts (4th February 1884). It consists of an Adagio leading to an Allegro moderato. Then follows an Intermezzo in the key of the relative minor. An Adagio (F major) leads to the Allegro Finale in D flat major. It is thus noticed in the *Musical Times* of March 1884 :—" Some listeners have professed to perceive in the work a deliberate intention to violate the established laws of form, but we confess that to us no such design is apparent. In matters of detail, Mr. Stanford shows himself an independent thinker, but in all essentials his newest work is as classical in outline as could possibly be desired. The opening Adagio is exceedingly impressive, and the succeeding Allegro moderato is worked out with splendid mastery of the subject-matter, the general effect being that of a lofty design carried into execution by a thoroughly experienced hand. The succeeding Allegro grazioso, a modified kind of Scherzo, is vigorous, and the final Allegro commodo, with its excellent first subject, seems scarcely less important than the first movement."

CHAPTER XI

SOME mention, however brief, must be made of various sonatas written by other contemporaries of the four composers discussed in the last chapter. After Beethoven, the only work which, from an evolution point of view, really claims notice is one by Liszt. All other sonatas are written on classical lines with more or less of modern colouring. Even M. Vincent d'Indy, one of the advanced French school of composers, has written a " Petite Sonate dans la forme classique."

Moscheles, in Germany, and Kalkbrenner, in France : these were once names of note. Their music is often clever and brilliant, but, to modern tastes, dry and old-fashioned ; much of it, too, is superficial.

Among still more modern works may be named those of Stephen Heller, Raff, Rubinstein, Bargiel, and Grieg. The sonatas of Heller are failures, so far as the name sonata means anything. He was not a composer *de longue haleine*, and his opening and closing movements are dull and tedious ; some

of the middle movements—as, for example, the two
middle ones of the Sonata in C major — are, however, charming.   Bargiel's Sonata in C major (Op.
34) is written somewhat in " Heller " style, but it is
stronger, and, consequently, more interesting than
any of that composer's.

Raff and Rubinstein both wrote pianoforte
sonatas, but these do not form prominent features
in their art-work.

Grieg's one Sonata in E minor (Op. 7) is a charming, clever composition ; yet as it was with Chopin,
so is it with this composer : his smallest works are
his greatest.

Of duet sonatas there is little more to do than
to mention the principal ones.   In the evolution of
the sonata they are of little or no moment.   Some,
however, are highly attractive.   It would be interesting to know who wrote the first sonata for four hands,
but the point is not an easy one to settle.   Jahn,
speaking of Mozart's duets, remarks that " pianoforte
music for two performers was then far from having
attained the popularity which it now possesses,
especially among amateurs."   We imagine that the

Sonate
à Quatre mains sur un Clavecin
Composé
par
J. C. Bach
———
à Amsterdam
chez J. Schnitt Marchand de Musique
dans le Warmoes-straat

was one of, if not the earliest. The part for the
second clavier is printed under that of the first.
The sonata consists of only two movements:
an Allegro and a Rondo. The general style and
treatment of the two instruments reminds one of
Mozart, but the music is crude in comparison.
Here is the commencement of the theme of the
first movement—

The duet sonatas of Mozart are full of charm
and skill, and will ever be pleasing to young
and old. Dussek has written some delightful
works, and Hummel's Op. 92, in A flat, is certainly
one of the best pieces of music he ever wrote.
Schubert's two sonatas (B flat, Op. 30; C, Op.
140) are very different in character: the one is
smooth and agreeable; the other contains some
of the noblest music ever penned by the composer.

Sonatinas are almost always written for educational purposes. No description, no analysis of
such works, is necessary; only a list of the best.
The "Twelve Sonatinas for the Harpsichord or
Pianoforte, for the use of Scholars" (Op. 12), by
James Hook (1746–1827), father of the well-
known humorist, Theodore Hook, deserve honour-
able mention. Each number contains only two

short movements; they are well written, and, though old, not dry. Joseph Bottomley, another English composer (1786–?), also wrote twelve sonatinas for the pianoforte.

Those of Clementi and Dussek seem destined to perennial life. The former composed twelve (Op. 36, 37, and 38), the latter six (Op. 20); and then, of course, of higher musical interest are the sonatinas of Beethoven (two) and Hermann Goetz (two). From an educational point of view, however, these are perhaps not of equal value with many others of inferior quality; but they are full of character and charm. Kuhlau (1786–1832), on whose name Beethoven wrote the well-known Canon, " Kuhl nicht lau," composed sonatas which, owing to their fresh, melodious character and skilful writing, justly take high rank. Op. 20, 55, 59, 60, and 88 have all been edited by Dr. H. Riemann. Among still more modern composers may be mentioned: Reinecke, whose three sonatinas (Op. 47), six sonatinas with " the right - hand part within the compass of five fingers " (Op. 127A), and (Op. 136) the " Six Miniature Sonatas " (another term for sonatinas) have given satisfaction to teachers, and enjoyment to many young pupils; also Cornelius Gurlitt, who has proved a prolific worker in this department of musical literature. His six sonatinas (Op. 121) and the duet sonatas (Op. 124,—really sonatinas) are exceedingly useful, and justly popular. Besides these, he has issued two series of progressive sonatinas: some by Diabelli, Pleyel, Steibelt, etc.; some from his own pen. Koehler's three sonatinas (without octaves), A. Loeschhorn's instructive sonatinas, E. Pauer's National Sonatinas (Ireland, Wales, Italy, etc.), and Xaver Scharwenka's two sonatinas are likewise of value.

Among various strange works written under the title of sonata we may count certain programme pieces. Thus, John Christian Bach, or "Mr. Bach," as he is named on the title-page, published a sonata "qui represente La Bataille de Rosbach," and an *N.B.* adds : " Dans cette Sonate La Musique vous montre le Comencement d'une Bataille le feu des Cannons et Mousqueterie L'Ataque de la Cavalerie et les L'Amendations des Blessées." This work consists of one movement (Allegro) in sonata-form. Except for the title, and the words "Canonade" and "Feu des Mousqueteries," it would be difficult to guess the subject. The music, which may be described as a study in the Alberti bass, is decidedly more correct in form than the French of the title-page. Then, again, Dussek composed a "Characteristic Sonata" describing "The Naval Battle and Total Defeat of the Grand Dutch Fleet by Admiral Duncan on the 11th of October 1797." But he was engaged in a much more suitable task when he wrote music *expressing the feelings* of the unfortunate Marie Antoinette.

There are three sonatas composed by A.

Quintin Buée.[1] No. 3 is "for two performers on one instrument." In the last movement, the first performer is " Le Français," and he rattles along with the popular tune " Ça ira," while the second, " The Englishman," steadily plays his national air, " Rule Britannia"; towards the close, *fors fuat*, " God save the King" and " Ça ira" are combined.

[1] He is described on the title-page as "formerly Composer to several Cathedral Churches in France." Buée's name is neither in Fétis nor the Pougin Supplément.

INDEX